Discovering
Saskatchewan Folklore

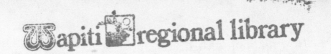

Discovering Saskatchewan Folklore

Three Case Studies
by Michael Taft

NeWest Press
Edmonton

First edition

Canadian Cataloguing in Publication Data

Taft, Michael, 1947-
Discovering Saskatchewan Folklore

ISBN 0-920316-76-X (bound). — ISBN 0-920316-74-3 (pbk.

1. Folklore - Saskatchewan. 2. Saskatchewan - Social life and customs. I. Title.
GR113.5.S3T33 1983   398'.097124   C83-091463-3

The research for this book was aided by the Saskatchewan Archives Board and the Saskatchewan Department of Culture and Recreation.

All photographs are by Michael Taft and are used with permission of the Saskatchewan Archives Board.

Credits:
Cover and design: Susan Colberg
Printing and Binding: Friesen Printers Ltd., Manitoba

Financial Assistance:
Alberta Culture
The Canada Council
Saskatchewan Arts Board

NeWest Publishers Ltd.,
204-8631-109 St., Edmonton, Alberta T6G 1E8

Contents

For My Parents,
Helen and Howard Taft

Preface

Since I have come to Saskatchewan, many people have asked me two questions: what is folklore and does Saskatchewan have folklore? The purpose of this book is to answer these two questions. If I have been successful, the reader will make a discovery: Saskatchewan has a wealth of folklore, which is all around us, if only we open our eyes and minds to it.

However, I have not attempted to write a survey of the traditions of this province. Such a work calls not for one slim book, but for many volumes. In fact, the task would be a never-ending one since the folklore of Saskatchewan is constantly growing and changing. Rather, I have presented three case studies of folklore which should give some indication of the scope of Saskatchewan's traditions. As well, these case studies should give the reader some ideas about how to discover folklore and lead to an understanding of what folklore is.

Thus, this study should be the first of many. Unlike other parts of North America, Saskatchewan has been slow to discover and appreciate its own traditions. The reasons for this are partly historical and partly social, but the time has come for the people of this province to collect and preserve their folklore, for such an activity is the sign of a mature culture that has pride and confidence in its heritage.

Folklore is perhaps the one natural resource in this province which has yet to be tapped; while it might not bring the monetary rewards of grain or potash, the discovery of Saskatchewan's folklore will do much to foster tolerance and understanding among the many groups which make up this province and, as well, will foster a "sense of community" among the people who call Saskatchewan their home. There is profit in studying folklore; there is loss in ignoring it.

The reader will notice that most of the folklore examples in this book have been transcribed verbatim from tape recordings. I have tried to let the people explain their traditions in their own words whenever possible, but the printed page cannot convey the expressiveness of the spoken word. None of us speak the same way we write. In our natural speech, we are often ungrammatical. We change our minds mid-way through sentences and then backtrack. We interrupt each other without regard for the proprieties of "complete sentences." We hem and haw, um and er, clear our throats, and make slips of the tongue.

In my transcriptions, I have tried to be as faithful to the spoken word as possible. However, I have not attempted to reproduce the accents or pronunciations of the speakers since such "dialect writing" is inevitably inaccurate and unflattering. On occasion I have omitted false starts and stuttering in the speech of those I've interviewed (quirks of speech we all share) in order to make the transcriptions more readable. But I have changed no words; nor have I changed sentence structure to make the transcriptions seem more like written language. The reader should keep this in mind and try to reconstruct the spoken word from its rather poor representation on the printed page.

In order to help the reader, I have inserted words and phrases enclosed in brackets to make clear certain spoken passages and to indicate certain non-verbal forms of communication. In other sections of the transcriptions, I have purposely left out digressions and irrelevant speech and have always replaced these with ellipses (. . .).

As do all folklorists, I have the people to thank for my work. Firstly, I thank those who took time from their everyday pursuits to teach me about their culture: Brian, Ed, Linda, Marcel and Mariette Buydens, Helga and Carl Christensen, Father Gilles Doucette, Joseph Greyeyes, Elsie and Wes Ingram, Jeannine Lebastard, and Bill Robertson. I also thank those others who have contributed their folklore to this book—Billy Bock, Anne Halderman, W.J. McIntyre, and Jim Young—as well as Barbara Cass-Beggs, whose fieldwork collections I have used. I also owe a debt of gratitude to several institutions and their workers: the Saskatchewan Archives Board, especially Douglas Bocking, Krzysztof Gebbard and D'Arcy Hande, the Multicultural Advisory Council of the Saskatchewan Department of Culture and Recreation, the Western Development Museum, especially Diana Mathews, the Shortt Collection of the University of Saskatchewan Library, and the Rt. Hon. John G. Diefenbaker Centre at the University of Saskatchewan.

1
What is Folklore?

Often, when I tell people that I am a folklorist, they assume that I study Indians or perhaps special ethnic groups. Rarely do they assume that I might be interested in them, no matter what their background or culture is. And yet I *am* interested in them, for just as the Indians and the immigrants have their own customs, traditions, and heritage, so too do all people. All people are "folk" and thus all people have folklore. The idea that "I don't have any folklore but other people do" is a common one and, especially in a province such as Saskatchewan where history is measured in years rather than in centuries, an understandable one. Often the most difficult traditions to see are those right under our noses.

The very common, obvious, and everyday nature of folklore gives it a certain obscurity. Like a fog, it is better seen at a distance than up close. And yet, if we detach ourselves for a moment from our culture and look back at it as would an outsider, our folklore would achieve a new-found clarity. We can easily see the folklore of the Indians because their culture is different from that of mainstream, European-based North American society. If we look even farther afield, folklore becomes even more noticeable: the traditions of an African tribe would undoubtedly stand out in relief to the eye of someone from Saskatchewan. In essence, the farther removed a culture is from our own, the easier it is for us to see their "strange" customs, habits, rituals, and general lore. However, if we imagine ourselves to be a member of this African tribe, think how strange the everyday activities of Saskatchewan people would seem. An African tribesman might very well say, "We don't have any folklore, but those weird people on the Canadian prairie are full of folklore."

Because folklore deals with common, everyday concerns rather than the activities or achievements of the famous, we tend to equate folklore with trivial or unimportant things. This misconception is a natural one, since for the most part we have been trained to look beyond our local and provincial borders, and beyond our own times, to see what is most significant. But perhaps it is time to look among ourselves and to take a more serious view of what has too often been taken for granted: our own folklore.

The general feeling that folklore is a product of simpler times and simpler people lies at the base of many misconceptions. Folklore is something to grow out of, something to look back on with nostalgia, something which marks the past. Interestingly, these same sentiments were held by our great grandparents and will undoubtedly persist for generations to come. Nostalgia never dies out. But nostalgia, as comforting as it may be, blinds us to the present cultural realities and, more dangerously, prevents us from seeing the unbroken flow of past, present, and future which we cannot escape. Our children are nostalgic about the 1960s and their children will look back to their roots in the ancient 1980s. Each generation looks back to the previous generation to discover (or define) its folklore, while ignoring their own, present-day traditions. The truth is that there have never been "simpler" times or "simpler" people than ourselves; human culture has always been, and will always be, infinitely complex and infinitely fascinating. Thus, whether one is young or old, urban or rural, highly educated or illiterate, a part of the mainstream culture or a member of some special enclave, one has folklore and one's folklore is inherently interesting and significant.

What then is folklore that it should command the respect and interest of all? A favourite "tradition" among folklorists is arguing over the exact definition of the word, since different people tend to put different boundaries around the field. Put simply, however, folklore is the common creativity of humankind. It is the way in which you and I are creative, clever, and artistic in our everyday lives. If there is one characteristic which separates us from other species, it is that we all need to express ourselves in symbolic, metaphoric, or just plain intelligent ways. We appreciate such activity in others as well as in ourselves and we practice this cleverness every day of our lives. Not everyone is an accomplished and acknowledged writer, musician, artist, or craftsman in his society, but everyone has the innate ability to share in these talents.

Thus, folklore examines the talents which we all possess and which we continually use. Of course, humans, being the resourceful creatures that they are, express their cleverness and artistry in a great many different ways. For the sake of convenience, however, we might view folklore as comprising five areas of creativity: verbal folklore, musical folklore, ritual, material folklore, and belief. But before we explore these areas, a word of warning: these categories are quite artificial, and the reality is that most items of folklore are more complex than this classification suggests. Indeed, almost any item of folklore might be viewed from the perspective of all five of these areas at once in order to get the fullest idea of how folklore operates within our everyday lives. But with this warning well-taken, let us look at these five areas of folklore.

Verbal folklore includes all the ways in which we use language in a creative or clever way. For example, if one could listen in at all the house visits and parties in Saskatchewan, all the community concerts, Christmas pageants, religious services and homecomings, all the get-togethers at the local pubs and corner stores, if one could eavesdrop on all the lonely farmers out in their fields, the housewives washing dishes or scrubbing floors, or even on all those who enjoy singing in the shower, one might come to understand one popular form of verbal folklore—songs and singing. There is no one who does not engage in this activity to some extent if only to join in on the chorus at a party or to sing Christmas carols or to celebrate someone's birthday with "Happy Birthday to You." Poetry is a fundamental part of human creativity, and song is the most common form of poetry in which we participate.

Verbal folklore also includes the stories which people tell. As with songs and poetry, stories are a form of creativity in which all people share, although some are known in their communities for being especially good raconteurs. Like songs, stories may be performed in a formal setting, such as during a speech before club members, or in an informal setting, such as during the visit of some neighbors. Stories may be elaborate and fanciful such as fairy tales, "strange but true" such as ghost stories, historical such as legends about past events (stories about John Diefenbaker or Louis Riel, for example), exaggerated such as tall tales, or absurd such as jokes.

There are even more common types of folktales. Even those who simply can't tell made-up stories, legends, or jokes have a large collection of personal experience stories: how one met one's spouse, most embarrassing moments, brushes with death, good or bad fortune, sexual experiences, one's memories of people who have died or of those far away, childhood experiences, and a multitude of other personal events which make up a lifetime and are told in the course of conversation. In addition, almost everyone has a sense of history, especially local history, and can usually tell stories about dramatic events and important happenings in their community: the great fire, who lived in the house on the hill, when electrification came in, the neighbor who achieved fame or infamy. Most of the stories in the third chapter are of this common, everyday variety.

But verbal folklore extends beyond the "literary" forms of poetry and tale to shorter, more conversational forms of creativity. Proverbs, proverbial exaggerations, maxims, sayings, and a whole range of clever use of language are a part of everyday speech. Indeed one would find it very difficult to communicate without the help of metaphors, similes, and aphorisms. Perhaps falling somewhere between the long forms of song and story and the short forms of proverb and saying is the riddle, another kind of verbal folklore, which is meant to test one's wit and humour.

Musical folklore often goes hand-in-hand with verbal folklore. The tune behind the songs and even the rhythm behind recitations and verses is a musical tradition which we all share. There are, of course, specialists in every community who can play the fiddle, guitar, piano, harmonica, zither, spoons or countless other instruments, but there is one instrument which we all play—the human voice. Whether we use our voice to hum simple tunes as we work or to give our clever use of language a "sing-song" quality (think of children's taunts), we are engaged in musical folklore. As well, most of us can whistle, tap our feet, clap our hands, and drum our fingers on a tabletop—all forms of music and rhythm which are so common that they are rarely given any thought. Most of us, as well, can use our bodies as rhythmic instruments to accompany music; that is, most of us can dance, however badly, given the proper situation. Thus, every country dance with a fiddler and a floor full of couples is a bit of musical folklore in which everyone, even the old man tapping his foot as he sits in the corner, participates.

Ritual, too, as a form of common creativity, is inescapable in our lives. At various times, we escape from the workaday patterns of everyday life—working, eating, relaxing, making love, and so on—and play a part in some communal celebration or some extraordinary event. Of course, as Shakespeare wrote, "all the world's a stage," and thus we are always playing one role or another, but when we become conscious of the role, when we know beforehand how we should respond to the playacting of others (that is, when we have a "script"), we perform a ritual.

The most overt kind of ritual is folk drama. The Christmas pageant, the party skit, and the school play are small dramas which are a part of many of our lives. As well, dressing up in costume, such as at Hallowe'en or for masquerade parties, is a form of folk drama. Closely allied to folk drama is play and games; the double-meaning of the word "play" is one indication of the closeness of these forms to each other.

Rituals also include the way we mark time—both personal time and the time represented by the calendar. Thus, whenever we personally achieve some new status in society, whenever we pass from one social level to another, we mark the occasion with a ritual. Birthdays are an annual ritual of this sort, but more important markers of personal time are rituals such as baptism, confirmation, graduation, marriage, promotion, initiation into clubs and societies, retirement, and the last ritual, the funeral.

We also mark the timespan of our community or culture. Look at any calendar and you will see certain days which call for celebration: New Year's Day, Easter, Victoria Day, Canada Day, Labour Day, Christmas, and many others. Some are religious, such as the pilgrimage to St. Laurent described in the fourth chapter; some are secular; some are celebrated by everyone, some by a small group; some are serious, some less so. What they all have in common is that at a specified time, the workaday activity of people in the community ends and everyone assumes a special role. Whether drama, game, ritual of passage, or calendar ritual, all these folklore forms involve common and communal creativity and artistry; "man the symbol-maker" is no better seen than in ritual folklore.

Man is also known as "the tool-maker." This characteristic of our species is best seen in material folklore, for we are also clever and artistic in the manipulation of our animal, vegetable and mineral surroundings. Much material folklore concerns crafts—the fashioning of utilitarian objects for everyday use. Before the Industrial Revolution, every community had its craftsmen: shoemakers, potters, blacksmiths, carpenters, coopers, bakers, butchers, tinsmiths, weavers, makers of musical instruments, and a host of other skilled artisans. However, many of these crafts have given way to mass production, and now most communities can boast few craftsmen. But craftsmen still exist as we see in the case of the Buydens in the fifth chapter, if in smaller numbers, and, like well-known local singers and raconteurs, these people are seen by the community as especially talented.

Material folklore takes in the large and the small. From the way we build our houses, barns, and churches to the kinds of clothes we wear, all are a part of our material folklore. But not all material folklore is utilitarian. Indeed many of the crafts that remain in our modern society represent a form of non-utilitarian creativity. The potter now shapes his vases, not simply to hold water, but to decorate a living room mantle. The metalworker has more on his mind when he fashions a belt buckle than holding up someone's pants. Hand-crafted items are now prized because of their relative rarity in this age of mass production, and have become objects of art perhaps more than objects of utility. Of course, there has always been a branch of material

16

folklore which is non-utilitarian—folk art. The making of items simply for aesthetic pleasure (which is, perhaps, utilitarian after all) is as old as mankind. In addition, the decorating of utilitarian objects, whether handmade or mass produced, seems a necessary activity in all cultures. We demand an adorned environment. Thus, folk artists abound, as we see in the many homes where the work of local painters is displayed on the walls.

The fifth area of folklore, belief, has a very different quality from the other four. Belief is not creative as such. We all have beliefs; indeed the way we view the world and the universe, what we think is "real" as opposed to imaginary, what is moral, what is the nature of "cause and effect"—in all, our general perceptions make up our "belief systems." These belief systems are shaped by our experiences, by what people tell us, and most importantly, by the culture in which we live. But again, belief is not in itself something creative.

However, we continually express our beliefs through creative acts, whether verbal, musical, ritual or material. Thus, proverbs express a belief through a verbally clever means. Religious music marks a certain religious belief system. A ritual such as the funeral tells much about the participants' beliefs concerning the dead. The shape of a church is a material representation of the parishoners' belief in a supreme being. Thus, this fifth area of folklore cuts across the other four areas to reveal the beliefs which we hold.

These are the five areas of folklore, yet they do not entirely explain the nature of this field. Verbal folklore, music, ritual, material folklore, and belief are the "lore" of folklore, but what about the "folk?" Of course we are all folk according to the definition put forth here, but we are all folk of different sorts. In other words, we all belong to different groups, and every group has its own special folklore. Indeed folklore helps to define and separate one group from another; in turn, each item of folklore is marked by the group in which it is found. For example, one kind of group to which most people belong is an occupational group, and each occupation has its own folklore: stories about foolish or clever workers, perhaps songs sung at company picnics or during labour troubles, rituals for greenhorns or initiates, specialized tools and other material items used on the job, beliefs about what causes good luck or bad luck in the work place, and many other traditions.

However, not all occupational groups share the same folklore. For instance, although many occupations have ritual pranks which they play on greenhorns, these activities will be specific to the type of work which the group performs. Thus, a greenhorn in a potash mine might be warned by an old-timer to keep an eye out for the salt rats. If the new miner falls for this trick by warily looking around, he can expect a good bit of laughter and ribbing at his expense. When he becomes an experienced miner, he might play this same trick on another generation of greenhorn workers. The greenhorn in a department store would not be warned about salt rats, however, since such a trick would be entirely out of context (that is, not a part of the occupational lore of sales clerks); rather, she might be sent to find a can of spotted paint for an impatient customer.

But the concept of group is a complex one, for at any given time a person belongs to many different groups: a family group, a religious group, a geographical group, an ethnic group, an occupational group, a racial group, an organization or club, a socio-economic group, a group sharing certain disabilities or physical similarities, as well as a number of other groups. For example, John Smith is a "Smith," a Roman Catholic, a native of Swift Current, a second-generation German-Canadian, a carpenter, a white man, a member of the local hockey team, a middle-class Canadian, and a weight-watcher. For each group he is a part of, he has a store of folklore which he shares with other group members.

Admittedly, folklore is an incredibly wide field. Is there anything which is *not* folklore? The simple but less useful answer is that all human creativity is indeed folklore. Dickens was simply a storyteller who used the printed word to relate his folktales. Rodin was a folk artist whose sculptures achieved some fame. Einstein's theories are simply another example of folk belief. And of course a case can be made for calling these men folk artists: Dickens' novels necessarily grow out of a storytelling tradition; Rodin's sculptures rest on a tradition of representing the human form which extends back beyond recorded history;

18

Einstein's theories grow out of centuries of modification of the traditional world view of western man. All three owe a debt to folklore.

But what distinguishes folklore is that it is not simply the creativity of people or of groups; such a definition would be so all-encompassing that it would be meaningless. Rather, the kind of creativity which people exhibit when they are involved in the everyday activities of small groups, communities, or localities is the stuff of folklore. Other forms of creativity—known sometimes as high-art culture and popular culture—transcend the boundaries of any one group or community and aim for a universal audience. Dickens, Rodin and Einstein are understood, appreciated and known by people far removed from the groups these geniuses belonged to. Old Uncle John who keeps track of the family history through his many stories is the folklore equivalent of Dickens; the woman in the community who makes designs and figures out of straw is the folklore equivalent of Rodin; the man who predicts local weather conditions by observing the activities of animals and the nature of plants is the folklore equivalent of Einstein. Folklore is truly "culture" with a small *c*. But the dividing-line between the world of folklore and the world of "high art" creativity is arbitrary and constantly shifting. All high art performers have their roots in their local traditions; all folk performers are influenced by creativity from outside their group and culture.

Folklore is the kind of creativity shared by members of a group; it helps to define the group and, in turn, is defined by the group. If this definition of folklore seems somewhat confusing, it is because of the subject: folklore cannot be pigeon-holed. It is a fluid, flexible subject of study whose boundaries only appear in one's peripheral vision and which can never be firmly grasped since these boundaries melt away at first touch. Yet folklore is the bedrock of all culture, and to understand folklore is to understand much about human creativity. To study folklore is to study ourselves.

2
What is
Saskatchewan Folklore?

Since everyone is a "folk", then most certainly there is folklore in Saskatchewan. Furthermore, in the light of the definition of folklore given in the previous chapter, the relatively recent European settlement of the province has no bearing on the question. As soon as people gather and consciously form a group—in this case a geo-political group called Saskatchewanites—they express, through their folklore, both their solidarity with each other and their differences from other groups.

But is the folklore of Saskatchewan different from that found in other places? Is there anything unique about the folklore of this province? Some would argue that Saskatchewan folklore is nothing more than a hodge-podge of traditions from other lands: that, except for the traditions of native people, the folklore of the province is simply a borrowing from older, more established cultures. Indeed this argument is voiced throughout the New World by those who see folklore as something ancient and unchanging. However, folklore is ever new, ever changing, while at the same time it is traditional and conservative. New World folklore has certainly grown out of the traditions of older cultures, but the New World landscape, climate, flora and fauna, as well as the social structures born in the New World, had an immediate effect on the Old World traditions of the settlers. The fact is that as soon as immigrants, whether French, English, Ukrainian, or Vietnamese, came to the New World, their folklore started to change and adapt itself to the new surroundings.

Saskatchewan is a unique part of the New World. In terms of landscape, it is different from both Alberta and Manitoba; in terms of social and political institutions, it is different from Montana and the Dakotas. Although it shares many of the same occupational and ethnic groups with its neighbors, the exact mixture and combination of these groups in Saskatchewan is unique. The effect of these factors on the Old World immigrant traditions is, therefore, bound to be unique, although somewhat subtly so to the untrained observer.

For example, when a Saskatchewan mother tells her child the story of *Cinderella*, she is certainly relying on a worldwide folktale tradition which is much older than the settlement of Saskatchewan. *Cinderella* has been told for hundreds of years among the cultures of Europe and Asia. Yet her telling will not be exactly like that of any other person in any other culture. Just as there are German variants, Turkish variants, and Chinese variants of the tale, so too are there Saskatchewan variants. The mother in Saskatchewan may give the story a certain agricultural flavour, insert a sense of morality into the story which fits twentieth-century Saskatchewan values, use modern and familiar names for the step-sisters, change the transformed animals into those recognized in this part of the world (gophers rather than lizards, perhaps), choose her own language structure and dialect in the telling, use facial expressions and body movements in a way unique to her and her culture—in short, adapt an international tale to her own particular Saskatchewan setting. Since no one country or culture can claim *Cinderella* as its own tale, all variants, including the Saskatchewan variants, are equally valid. Thus, if Saskatchewan cannot claim that all of its folklore is unique and indigenous to the province (what culture can?), it can certainly claim unique and indigenous variants upon international folklore forms.

Some adaptations, of course, are less subtle than those which have occurred in the Saskatchewan *Cinderella*. Take Ukrainian traditions. There are, in fact, no Ukrainian traditions in Saskatchewan; there are, instead, Ukrainian-Canadian or Ukrainian-Saskachewan traditions. The designs on Ukrainian-Saskatchewan Easter eggs do not conform in every respect to those found in the Ukraine: certain wheat motifs common here are less common or nonexistent in the Ukraine; the symbolism of the designs recognized in the Ukraine is often disregarded or unknown to many egg designers in Saskatchewan. The twelve meatless dishes of the Ukrainian Christmas feast are retained by many in this province, but the nature of the food and its preparation are different from that in the Ukraine. The regional identity of Ukrainian dancers' costumes has become mixed and less meaningful among Ukrainian-Saskatchewan people than they were in Hutsul or Bukovyna. Perhaps the greatest adaptation has occurred in the Ukrainian language which, from the moment the immigrants arrived in Canada, started to change and diverge from the mainstream tongue of those Ukrainians who remained in Europe. The adaptations which have occurred in Ukrainian immigrant folklore have also occurred in the folklore of all other immigrants to this province, whether the traditions were European, American, or even Manitoban in origin.

But Saskatchewan folklore is also unique in another way. Although all cultures borrow from the great international storehouse of traditions—tales, songs, rituals, foods, and the like—not all cultures borrow the same group of folklore items from this storehouse. Thus, for whatever reasons, the people of Saskatchewan may tell certain fairy tales more often than others, or may not tell some fairy tales at all, even though all the world's international fairy tales (*Cinderella, Rumpelstiltskin,* and so on) are theoretically available to those in the province. Each culture picks and chooses the world's traditions according to a formula which is entirely unique to that culture; once these traditions are chosen, they are adapted and changed to fit the needs, aesthetics, and social situations found in that culture.

Does Saskatchewan have unique folklore? As with so many questions concerning folklore, the answer is "yes and no." Saskatchewan can no more escape from the great storehouse of world traditions than it can escape from the world itself; yet Saskatchewan can no more prevent its own peculiar adaptations and changes to these traditions than it can control its own history and mixture of people. Just as folklore is both old and new at the same time, it is both international and regional at the same time.

As a general example of this paradox, consider the song and poetry traditions of Saskatchewan. Are they unique and indigenous to the province? If one could gather the complete repertoires of folksong and poetry from everyone in Saskatchewan, one would undoubtedly find that most of the songs sung in the province were composed elsewhere— British ballads, American country songs, Canadian popular songs, and the like—and most of the poems and recitations would likewise come from beyond Saskatchewan's borders— Robert W. Service poems, verses from school readers, internationally known skipping rhymes, and so on.

Of course, it would be impossible to conduct such a large survey, but the repertoire study of a single singer is possible and might reveal the nature of Saskatchewan's folksong traditions. One such singer is Jeannine Lebastard of Eastend. She was born in the French-Saskatchewan community of Dollard, both of her parents having come from Northern France. As a young girl in the 1920s and 1930s, she learned French songs from her mother and English songs from school friends and the newspapers. Over the years, her repertoire of songs has grown to several hundred which she has carefully written down and kept in three songbooks— one for French songs and two for English songs. At parties or when relaxing with family and friends, Jeannine is likely to bring out these songbooks and entertain the group with her singing. The songbooks help her to remember the words of the songs and also allow others to request songs from Jeannine's repertoire; in this sense, the songbooks are a physical manifestation of Jeannine's memories and traditions which all her friends and family can share.

But the songbooks are also useful for the type of repertoire study mentioned above. What kind of songs does Jeannine Lebastard sing? A survey of her songbooks reveals that nearly all of the songs originated outside of Saskatchewan: well-known French folksongs such as "Le Chevalier du Guet" and "C'est l'Aviron Qui Nous Mene," a few Irish and British ballads such as "The Butcher Boy" and "Gypsy Rover," some Canadian and American ballads such as "Rescue from the Moose River Gold Mine" and "Birmingham Jail," sentimental songs such as "The Letter Edged in Black" and "Drunkard's Child," a good number of old popular hits such as "My Darling Clementine" and "Darktown Strutter's Ball," and many country music standards such as "Red River Valley" and "Rose of San Antone" (and many Wilf Carter songs).

Perhaps representative of Jeannine's repertoire of non-Saskatchewan songs is "Little Marian Parker," an American sentimental ballad about the 1927 kidnapping and murder of a Los Angeles banker's child:

Little Marian Parker

Way out in California a family bright and gay
Was planning for their Christmas not very far away

They had a little daughter a sweet and pretty child
And all the folks who knew her love Marian Parker's smile

She left her home one morning for school not far away
And no one dreamt that danger could come to her that day

And then the murderer villain a friend with heart of stone
Took little Marian Parker away from friends and home

The world was horror-stricken and people held their breath
Until they found poor Marian her body cold in death

And then they caught the coward young Hickman was their
man
They brought him back to justice his final trial to stand

There is a great commandment that says, "Thou Shalt Not
Kill"
And all those who do not heed it their cups of sorrow fill

This song should be a warning to parents far and near
We cannot guard too closely the ones we love so dear[1]

Although "Little Marian Parker" is clearly an American song, Jeannine's version, like local versions of *Cinderella*, is a Saskatchewan variant; no one else sings the song in exactly the same way as does Jeannine. Her style of presentation is her own. As well, either wittingly or unwittingly, she has altered words, phrases, and stanzas in her singing. For example, the usual phrase which describes the murderer is "a *fiend* with heart of stone," but either by mistake or by design,

Jeannine has substituted the word "friend" for "fiend"; in addition, she has omitted a stanza concerning the details of Hickman's trial, which is found in other versions of the song.

But Jeannine's songbooks also reveal the kind of "picking and choosing" discussed earlier which marks one culture's folklore from another. Although most of her songs are a part of the general storehouse of North American traditional songs, her particular selection marks her as a resident of Saskatchewan. Thus, there is a preponderance of songs with western settings and, more specifically, songs about the cowboy and ranching life—an occupation which not only marks Saskatchewan but particularly the southwest corner of the province where ranching is more prevalent than farming. The following songs are only a few of those in Jeannine's repertoire with this western, ranching orientation: "Strawberry Roan," "Roll Along Prairie Moon," "When the Work's All Done this Fall," "Cowboy's Dream," "Round-Up Time in Texas," "Twilight on the Prairie," "Springtime in the Rockies," "Take Me Back to My Boots and Saddle," "Home on the Range," "Cowboy Jack," "Texas Plains," "A Bridle on the Wall," "Cowboy's Sweetheart," "Ride Tenderfoot Ride," "Old Chisolm Trail," "Beautiful Girl of the Prairies," "Get Along Little Doggies," and "Little Old Sod Shanty on the Plain." As with "Little Marian Parker," Jeannine makes each of these songs a Saskatchewan variant of a North American song.

There are many singers in Saskatchewan and many of them also keep songbooks. Their repertoires are probably not too different from Jeannine's (with the exception of her French songs) and they also sing Saskatchewan variants of their songs. However, the kind of variations discussed so far are largely unconscious or unwitting—they are the result of contact with a specific culture which inevitably shapes all outside traditions. Yet Saskatchewan singers and composers are not above consciously altering some traditional songs to make them fit the Saskatchewan context better. In essence, many Saskatchewan singers "localize" certain songs in order to make them significant to the region. Take the following Ontario song as an example:

The Poor Lone Girl of Ontario

I make a complaint of a plaguey pest,
Known by the name of the Great North-West
This wondrous land of the setting sun
Has taken my beaux away, every one.

Chorus:
One by one, they have all cleared out
Thinking to better themselves, no doubt;
Caring little how far they go
From the poor lone girl of Ontario

First I was sweet on Johnny L. Brown,
The nicest young fellow in all the whole town;
But he said good-bye, and sailed away
And now he's settled in Thunder Bay.

Next, I was fishing for Farmer Lee's Dick,
Thought him so dull that he couldn't cut a stick.
But he waved his hat with a hip, hip hurrah!
And said he was going to Manitobaw.

Fat little, plump little Johnny Gray—
I hinted we better get spliced, and stay.
He said to me, "That's rather too thin."
And he turned his toes to Kee-watin.

Mine Dutchman lover, Hans Ritter von Krout—
So lame he could hardly escort me out;
With magic ointment he greased his leg,
And slid to the city of Winnipeg.

The long lean druggist with specs on his nose—
I thought that this fellow would soon propose;
But he sold his bottles and he was gone
Clean away to Saskatchewan.

Jim Bambridge, the blacksmith's son,
Of all my beaux, the very best one—
Put on an excursion got up very pretty,
And he's gone off to Rapid City.

I'll sling my goods in a carpet sack,
I'm off to the West, and won't come back.
I'll have a husband and a good one too,
If I have to follow him to Cariboo![2]

When Ontarians migrated to Saskatchewan in the late nineteenth century, they brought this song with them. Indeed this comic song concerns the migration itself. However, in at least one case, a Saskatchewan-born child of these early immigrants took the song and localized it to fit a more modern Saskatchewan context. Anne Halderman of Shaunavon learned the song from her mother, but altered the song in the following manner:

A Poor Lone Girl in Saskatchewan

Oh have you not heard of that plaguey pest
That's known by the name of the Great North West
For that wondrous land of the setting sun
Has taken my beaux away one by one

Chorus:
For one by one they have all cleared out
Hoping to better themselves no doubt
Caring but little how far they have gone
From a poor lone girl in Saskatchewan

First I was sweet on a man named Len
He owned a good farm but he had a yen
To see the Peace Country and try his luck
Now he's at Grande Prairie and here I'm stuck

There was dear Billie Mack now I thought OK
I hinted he'd better get spliced and stay
But he said to me, "Though I think you're pretty
I have urgent business in Dawson City"

My lover Ern Seifert has rheumatiz
In spite of that I was bound to be his
But with Rawleigh's Liniment he cured his ache
And soon he was headed for Great Bear Lake

Then there was Black Bob oh what a catch
I though it would be the perfect match
But he seemed in no hurry to take a wife
Now he's prospecting in Yellowknife

I've made reservations with T.C.A.
I'm off to the North and I'm going to stay
I won't give up till I've found a mate
If I have to follow him to Bering Strait[3]

Although the theme of these two songs is the same—the departure of eligible males for points west—Anne Halderman altered the song to fit her place and time. To her mother, the west meant Northern Ontario, Manitoba, and Saskatchewan; to Anne, the west meant Alberta, the Northwest Territories, and the Yukon. Just as nineteenth-century men migrated to the prairies to find their fortune, twentieth-century Saskatchewan men have gone to frontiers further north and west. Ironically, the Ontario heroine's idea of remoteness is the Cariboo—a place which seems close at hand to the Saskatchewan girl; *her* idea of a remote location takes her to the very edge of the continent—the Bering Strait. Thus, Anne Halderman altered the place names to fit twentieth-century migration patterns.

But Anne altered this song in other ways, which make the song even more relevant to her region. Whereas the names of the men in the Ontario song, if they ever referred to actual people, were meaningless to a young girl in Shaunavon, Billie Mack, Ern Siefert and the others in the Saskatchewan song were men from Anne Halderman's community. She used one of the most traditional ways of making a nationwide song regional: by inserting the names of friends and neighbors, she gave the song special significance to both her and to her audience. In addition, she made the song more familiar to her time period by referring to Trans-Canada Airways—a phenomenon of the mid twentieth century, rather than the late nineteenth century.

Is Anne Halderman's song, then, a part of Ontario folklore or Saskatchewan folklore? It is, of course, related to both in terms of its general poetic structure and its theme. Both parts of the country experienced outmigration at different times in their history, and thus the song is significant to both Ontario and Saskatchewan. But Anne's song grew out of and apart from the Ontario song tradition and shows all the signs of being part of Saskatchewan's cultural heritage.

Theme is a great unifying factor in the folklore of different cultures. The universality of the theme of "Little Marian Parker"—Thou Shalt Not Kill—makes the song at home equally in Saskatchewan and California. Thus, it is not surprising that traditional themes find their way into local songs and local song variants. Another example of a national or international song made local is the well-known parody of the hymn "Beulah Land" in which the singer describes his homeland as something short of "paradise." This parody is sung and enjoyed in all three prairie provinces and in the plains states of the United States, but in each location the words are altered to describe in more precise detail the particular "paradise" of the singer. Known by such names as "O Prairie Land," "Sweet Dakota Land," "Sweet Kansas Land," "Sweet Nebraska Land," "Alberta Land," and "Saskatchewan," the song belongs to no place and every place as its form shifts and changes to fit each location. The following stanzas are from the Nebraska version:

Sweet Nebraska Land

Ah Nebraska Land, Sweet Nebraska Land,
As on thy burning soil I stand,
I look away across the Plains
And wonder why it never rains.

We've reached the land of desert sweet
Where nothing grows for man to eat
And the wind it blows with fev'rish heat
Across the plains so hard to beat.

We have no wheat, we have no oats,
We have no corn to feed our shoats;
Our chickens are so very poor,
They beg for crumbs outside the door.

Our horses are of bronco race;
Starvation stares them in the face.
We do not live, we only stay,
'Cause we're too poor to move away.[4]

The Saskatchewan version shares some of the same sentiments, but allusions to the bitter cold, and to the East especially, make this variant a part of Saskatchewan's folklore:

Saskatchewan

Saskatchewan, the land of snow,
Where winds are always on the blow,
Where people sit with frozen toes.
And why we stay here no one knows.

Chorus:
Saskatchewan, Saskatchewan,
There's no place like Saskatchewan,
We sit and gaze across the plains,
And wonder why it never rains,
And Gabriel blows his trumpet sound,
He says: "The rain, she's gone a-round."

Our pigs are dyin' on their feet,
Because they have no feed to eat,
Our horses, though of bronco race,
Starvation stares them in the face.

The milk from cows has ceased to flow,
We've had to ship 'em East, you know,
Our hens are old and lay no eggs,
Our turkeys eat grasshopper legs.

But still we love Saskatchewan,
We're proud to say we're native ones,
So count your blessings drop by drop,
Next year we'll have a bumper crop.[5]

Indeed parody is one way in which songs become localized. In the above songs, the singers might not necessarily be aware of the relationship between their song and "Beulah Land," since the songs can stand very well on their own. However, some parodies demand more knowledge of the "straight" song from which they grew in order to be fully appreciated. Here the alteration of a nationwide tradition to fit a specific area is a very conscious process. For example, Jeannine Lebastard sings a song which she entitles "Just a Parody." The very title alerts us to the localization of a well-known song. In this case, the straight song is "Springtime in the Rockies" (which Jeannine also sings) and undoubtedly most people in her community know and consciously compare the parody with this popular song. This parody, like "Saskatchewan," dwells on the plight of the prairie farmer:

Just a Parody

I'm sitting in my shack out on the prairie
I never even flinch when prices drop
The torrid winds and drought, the worms and hoppers
Have played the very mischief with my crop

Chorus:
When it's springtime on the prairie
I'll be nought but skin and bone
When again the flowers are blooming
You can almost hear my groan
Once again I'll risk my seed wheat
And I'll labour all the day
For I'm a dry-land farmer
With a load of debts to pay

I'm tired of eating horse's hump and thistles.
I think I'd like to try a piece of cake
The only thing I've got in my stomach
Is just a solemn empty ache

We never have much fruit upon the prairie
I hoped I'd never see another prune
But now a prune might be as sweet or sweeter
Than any bride you ever see in June

Chorus

They talk of shipping beans in by the carload
I don't like beans but anything will do
There ain't no brute that I could cut a steak from
Nor one that I could make a dandy stew

Sometimes I think that I will never winter
My clothes are thinner than a Scotsman's cream
The hoard of pennies saved in times of childhood
Would look just now more like a miser's dream

Chorus

I hear that in the East they're wearing shorties
But even then I am short of shorts
And if I tried to work among the thistles
I am afraid I'd be all out of sorts

They say overalls will be in fashion
But that won't make me up to date for formal balls
For I'm in an awful bad condition
I haven't got a suit that covers all

Chorus

Although both "Saskatchewan" and "Just a Parody" owe their existence to songs from other parts of the world, one can easily see how much a part of Saskatchewan these songs are. Both songs reveal the strong agricultural base of the province, and in their way express the worries and frustrations of farming in Saskatchewan. Both hearken back to the earlier history of the province when the settlers struggled to turn prairie land into farm land; as well, both songs remind us of the poverty and despair of the Great Depression which combined with the dust bowl conditions of the 1930s to make the Saskatchewan farmer's lot among the worst in North America. In addition, both songs take somewhat subtle swipes at the East, which until recent times was the symbol of prosperity and which has always been seen by prairie people as the exploiter of the economy of the disadvantaged West. That these songs are still known and sung in Saskatchewan, despite the current prosperity of the province and its people, tells us much about the Saskatchewanite's sense of history and how the people of this province see themselves in relation to other regional groups.

So far the songs discussed all have their sources outside of Saskatchewan and therefore show the links between this province's heritage and that of other areas. However, there are also songs and poems which are, in every sense, homegrown, which owe their existence entirely to the specific circumstances in which the people of Saskatchewan find themselves. These local songs (as opposed to "localized" songs) grow out of particular incidents in the province's history, the accomplishments of citizens of Saskatchewan, and the political and social concerns of the people. Taken together, these local songs explain what it means to live in this province; the songs are a running commentary on the lives of the people of Saskatchewan.

One kind of local song might best be described as an anthem, a song which praises a particular locality and shows the allegiance of the people to the place in which they live. Unlike "Saskatchewan," which is perhaps a mock-anthem, these songs are serious and often sentimental. The following song, sung by Jeannine Lebastard, is an anthem for Eastend. "Where the White Mud River Flows" was written by a soldier away from home and expresses his nostalgia and homesickness for Eastend, Saskatchewan:

Where the White Mud River Flows

There's a river that is flowing towards a southern sea
'Tis not famed in song or story still it's good enough for me
It called me from the southlands where the cherry blossoms
grow
And I'll settle down forever where the White Mud River flows

Chorus:
Where the White Mud River is flowing
Where the pretty bluebells bloom
Where the prairie are a-glowing
Where the beauty of the rose
Where the summer sun is shining
No one sits down there repining
Each day has a silver lining
Where the White Mud River flows

In a little land-thatched cabin beyond the southern sea
Where I hope to live my life out when this cruel war is o'er
May then life deal kindly with me and war's troubles and
woes
Be to me a bleating memory where the White Mud River
flows

Chorus

We come from every nation from this great and glorious West
To uphold the flag of Britain we have sent our very best
And no foreigner's foot can trample on our pretty prairie rose
'Tis the emblem of our country where the White Mud River
flows

Chorus

If I get a final summons from the courthouse in the sky
From the judge of all the nations he may deem it no surprise
If I ask him just one favour he may grant it no one knows
Take me back to dear old Eastend where the White Mud
River flows

Chorus[6]

Like most local songs, "Where the White Mud River Flows" alerts us to the fact that in Saskatchewan there are groups within groups; every area of the province has its own traditions and, in turn, every community in these areas has its own folklore. Like all regions, Saskatchewan is an amalgamation of smaller groups, all of whom owe some kind of allegiance to a wide and diverse region. Thus, the above anthem is not simply a part of Saskatchewan folklore, but also a part of Eastend folklore.

Indeed most local songs concern the specific community in which they are sung, rather than the province as a whole. An incident, a local character, a political or social development triggers a composer to write and sing a local song. For example, the White Mud River, which is officially known as Frenchman's Creek, has given rise to another local song. In 1952 the river overflowed its banks and flooded Eastend and the surrounding area. This natural catastrophe inspired a comic ballad by William Bock. Billy

Bock, as he was best known, was well-known in Eastend for his satirical songs and poems as well as his humorous writings. Perhaps because the flood caused no loss of life nor any permanent damage to the region, Bock could make light of the catastrophe in his satirical style:

Frenchman's Creek

I've been asked to sing a little song to you
About the Eastend flood in '52
Here's a song that the neighbors will never forget
In fact quite a few of us are still all wet

Well I met Corky Jones on the Chimney Coulee Trail
He'd been out putting salt on a dinosaur's tail
He was humped in the saddle half-covered with mud
And he said, "Boys get ready for a big-time flood"

Chorus:
Because the water is high rolling down the Frenchman
Snow's deep in the Cypress Hills
The flats they were flooded all the way to Robsart
The farmers up the valley had to move their stills

'Twas the middle of April and the night was cold
The lightning was flashing and the thunder rolled
You could tell by the roar and the spray in the sky
The Frenchman River was running high

Well the gates in the dam they were opened up wide
It came over the top and around both sides
It kept on rising and it rose some more
'Twas a mile and a half from shore to shore

Chorus

Now the mayor of the town he was up all night
He was often wrong but his name was Wright
The council decided to prepare for the worst
They would save all the women and the children first

They blew the siren and they rang the bell
When it looked like everything was going to hell
For the river was running eleven thousand second-feet
There was four feet of water going down Main Street

Chorus

Well the women and the children they were all afloat
We gathered five hundred of them up by boat
We tallied them out and we never lost one
Well we herded them all over to Shaunavon

Those Shaunavon people they were sure ace-high
They made them welcome and they got them dry
They fed them well and they bedded them down
And they gave them the keys to the doggone town

Chorus

When the peak came down the Cypress Hills
The houses were shifting on their sills
Old Noah looked down from Cypress Park
Said, "I wish I could remember where I left my ark"

When the dam went out with a rush and a roar
A wall of water from shore to shore
Those railroad tracks somebody told me
They were later recovered down at Val Marie

Chorus

Benny Rose was washing out his old red socks
Paul Bunyan came along on his ink-blue ox
Said Paul to Benny, "It's a damp wet day
But I'd sure like to buy me some alfalfa hay"

Old Babe looked up with a hungry eye
When a stack of alfalfa went a-sailing by
Said Benny to Paul, "If it's not too high
I'd like to swap you that one for a bottle of rye"

Chorus

Now the dam's been rebuilt and the water's gone down
They've graded up the streets in the valley town
The fields are green from shore to shore
But we hope the old river never plays an encore

Chorus[7]

The local nature of this song is evident beyond the recounting of the flood. Like many good local songwriters (remember Anne Halderman), Bock has included the names of friends and neighbors in his song to make the entire composition more familiar to the people of Eastend. In addition, Bock pokes fun at the mayor and other citizens of the town in a kind of kidding fashion which goes on constantly among community members. This easy kidding, which might be resented if it came from an outsider, shows that Bock is a part of the community which he sings about. "Frenchman's Creek" was composed by a community member for community members, and is a perfect example of a local song.

Just as extraordinary events are grist for the local composer's mill, so are the doings of extraordinary members of the community. Another song commemorates a local invention which delighted and intrigued the people of Swift Current. In the late 1940s, W.J. McIntyre decided to build a mechanical horse. His invention, dubbed Blowtorch, was a black and white, stiff-legged metal horse with an internal gas engine. For the amusement of his fellow citizens, McIntyre would ride Blowtorch down the street. But McIntyre's creativity did not stop there; to commemorate his invention, he wrote the following song:

Blowtorch

Give me a steel horse the old farmer cried
So a hammer and wrench will fix his inside
A hoss that eats fuel as hot as the sun
That burns up our hay before it's begun.

Chorus:
Here comes Blowtorch, blowing smoke and flame
Dancing, prancing iron horse, flowing tail and mane
Coming down the home stretch, parading thru the town
None can touch old Blowtorch for miles and miles around

And oh for a horse that doesn't eat hay
The fair damsel cried, now Dobbin's away:
A sweet smelling horse, a stableman's dream
No trick to keep the barn and city streets clean

Chorus[8]

37

One of the greatest sources for the local poet and song-writer is community politics and squabbles, and every town and village in the province has its share of social controversy. While much of the debate over the actions of local politicians, the decisions of city councilors, the growth of local industry, and the general changes in the lifestyle of the community occur over the back fence and in the corner store, these issues are also raised in local poetry and song. A search of community papers reveals many examples of this form of poetry. Billy Bock composed a song in this vein over the controversy of the installation of sewer lines in Eastend—the topic lent itself easily to Bock's sense of humour and satirical style. Note that he again pokes fun at the local citizenry as only an insider can:

The Civil War

Eastend was once a happy town where harmony and love
Was busting out at all the seams and in the trees above
The doves of peace would lay eggs, there was no sign of strife
For each man loved his neighbor and sometimes his
neighbor's wife

But a sudden change soon came about, storm clouds were in
the sky
Nobody stopped to kiss a body coming through the rye
For each man eyed his neighbor with malice and with hate
Housewives no longer spilled the beans across the garden
gate

Chorus:
We had a war, a civil war
Folks often asked us what we all were fighting for
Well most of us wanted water mains and sewers and bathtubs
too
But the rest of us decided they'd make the slop pails do

It was sewer pipes versus slop pails, the town was split in two
With profane propaganda the air was often blue
The sewer-and-water faction had a sanitary plank
They said shallow wells and slop pails and toilets always
stank

Chorus

38

But those slop-pailers were stubborn, they fought with tooth
and nail
They said our nitwit council should be languishing in jail
Well they told how high taxation and plumber union fees
Would land us in the poorhouse and they'd throw away the
key

Chorus

But when the vote was counted, those slop-pailers met defeat
And drag-lines started tearing up our quiet village street
And peace and harmony once more displaced the grapes of
wrath
So when next you visit Eastend, just stop in and have a bath[9]

Thus, the local events of everyday life have been the
source for countless songs and poems in Saskatchewan. But
two more examples show how the particular ethnic mixture
of peoples in the province has also led to home-grown,
indigenous traditions of song and poem. Because
Saskatchewan is a land of immigrants and thus a land of
many languages, the province's folklore reflects this fact of
ethnicity in its use of immigrant themes and immigrant
languages. Although the immigrants brought their poetic
traditions with them from the Old World, these traditions,
like all other parts of their culture, were immediately
transformed by the new land. Thus, in Saskatchewan there is
a tradition of songs and poems about the immigration
experience and about the settling of the new land. These
works, though echoing the poetic heritage of other countries,
are entirely a part of Saskatchewan's cultural landscape. The
following translation is from a long poem about the history
of the Bekevar Hungarian settlers who came to the Kipling
area at the turn of the century:

160 acres were given for 10 dollars
they asked 25 dollars for a cow,
the price of a calf was 5 or 6 dollars.
When the weather turned cold
thousands of acres were all around
and grass grew everywhere.
The poor man who acquired land

had no money for the boards [to build] a house.
Someone then figures it out
and brought the wood from the woods.
The others followed his example.
One after the other built his house
nicely plastering the attic
and putting the ploughed-down prairie, the earth on top.
The making of such a house
cost 15 or 20 dollars.
Although the rain came in in summer
in winter it was good warm.
There, happiness was great
when they could move into the dirt-covered house
saying grace to the Lord . . .[10]

Such a poem is a historical document for the Hungarian settlers, but it is also the document of a group which is in the process of acculturation—making itself a part of the fabric of Saskatchewan. As such groups become more and more a part of the larger community and as they come into increasing contact with members of other ethnic groups, their traditions begin to reflect these new contacts and "incursions" into their group. Thus today, Ukrainian-Canadian fiddlers include Irish jigs in their repertoires, while people of non-Slavic background send their children to Ukrainian dance school and eat perogies for dinner. These strange ethnic mixtures also mark Saskatchewan's folk culture.

But even before the great migrations from Europe, there was a kind of ethnic mixing in Saskatchewan. The following song is an example of this phenomenon, in that its chorus is part Cree and part English. In its small way, this song reveals the early contact between Indian and white man in nineteenth-century Saskatchewan simply by its merger of the languages of these two groups. The song, "The Mounted Police Recruit," is, of course, also a part of the folklore of an occupational group with strong roots in Saskatchewan: The Royal Canadian Mounted Police. But the fact that it includes Cree words in its chorus makes this song more than simply an in-group piece of folklore. The history of contact between the native people and the RCMP is indeed a checkered one, but that the contact was significant to both groups is revealed in the very existence of this song among the RCMP.

That the song was apparently a favourite of the police at the time of the Northwest Rebellion in 1885 adds further significance to the English-Cree chorus, with the historical conflict seemingly reflected in the conflict of languages within the song. Note as well that the song is a protest song or a song well-suited to grumbling recruits. As with the local songs of Billy Bock, this occupational song makes fun of those within the group—a song which outsiders could never have composed or sung. As well, the song is a practical joke on greenhorn recruits who might not yet understand the Cree; to ask the meaning of the words is to reveal one's ignorance of the group's traditions. The Cree words may be roughly translated as follows: *Shemagonish* is policeman or soldier; *mistahe soneyas* means "a lot of money"; and *neyaninosap ta twabisk* means "fifteen dollars."

The Mounted Police Recruit

Being out of work while down below,
I had no other place to go;
Friends and pals not on the increase
So I went and joined the Mounted Police.
We shipped on board the C.P.R.
Each one thanking his lucky star,
The medical test successfully passed,
Each with a government job at last.

Chorus:
Come on and join the Shemagonish outfit,
It's mistahe soneyas pay
Get neyaninosap ta twabisk a month,
That's just fifty cents a day.

At Regina we arrived one noon
And learned to use the shovel and broom;
Then they hustled us out upon the square,
The balance or goose-step to prepare.
'Twould curdle the milk in any churn
To hear Pat Mahoney's "Right about turn,"
And "Point your toes, hold up you head."
Till all the men wished they were dead.

Chorus

At the riding school we fared as bad
Without the saddle we wished we had.
While veterans looked on with satisfied sneer,
To see some coyote pitched on his ear.
We'd ride a bronco that would buck and jump,
With a shoulder stick set to straighten our hump.
The boys all cried, "Stay with him Pat;"
"Get on there coyote, I'll hold your hat."[11]

Thus we see that Saskatchewan does have its own indigenous folksongs and poems. Yet we must not lose sight of the basic characteristics of folklore: it is both old and new, both international and regional, at one and the same time. Though local songs are, by definition, locally composed, their themes and poetic styles are a part of the greater, world-wide tradition. Thus, there are many ballads about floods, many anthems to small localities, many songs which make fun of local politics, not only in Saskatchewan, but in all parts of the world. Saskatchewan composers share their themes with many others. Likewise, the poetic structure, the metre, and the rhyme scheme of the local songs are traditional to all parts of the English-speaking world. If the Saskatchewan composers have discovered new topics for songs, they have nevertheless chosen to write these songs in traditional poetic styles. As well, the music of these songs is made up of tunes and mixtures of tunes which traditional singers from many different regions have used; making up a new tune is much more difficult than making up new words.

The greater tradition is also seen in some of the allusions and phrases used in these local songs. Composers quite naturally draw on the general storehouse of knowledge in writing their local songs. For example, Bock's "The Civil War" alludes to the Scottish song, "Comin' Through the Rye," while his "Frenchman's Creek" includes the traditional tall tale characters of Paul Bunyan and his blue ox, Babe; the "fair damsel" in "Blowtorch" seems to hearken back, quite consciously, to old English ballads and romantic stories.

Does Saskatchewan have its own folklore? The answer is that this province has no more and no less of an indigenous heritage than any other region. It borrows no more and no less than any other area from the great storehouse of folklore; it changes and adapts traditions no more and no less than any other region. Saskatchewan cannot help but have its own folklore, but it also cannot help but share in the folklore of other areas and cultures. Perhaps one final example will illustrate many of the points made in this chapter. A few years ago, Bill Robertson from Shaunavon told me a joke. He had heard it in his home town around 1970 and had undoubtedly told it on and off since then as a part of his considerable repertoire of jokes. At my request, he wrote the joke down:

First guy: *Well Jake, what would you do if you won the lottery?*

Farmer: *Well, farm till it was all gone I guess.*

This joke certainly has all the earmarks of a home-grown Saskatchewan joke. Like the songs, "Saskatchewan" and "Just a Parody," it tells of the plight of the poor dry-land farmer who is bound to remain broke no matter what happens. Is there anything closer to the historical perception which the people of Saskatchewan have of themselves? Yet soon after hearing Bill's joke, I read another version of the same joke:

It is said by loggers that a wealthy man once went into the streets of Portland, Oregon, to see if he could find a likely recipient for some charitable assistance. He stopped people randomly on the street, asking them what they would do if he were to give them a million dollars. He stopped one young man who said, "Now, if I had a million dollars, I'd buy myself a big house, some fancy cars, and I'd be able to get married and live in high style." This didn't satisfy the charitable intentions of the millionaire, so he looked further, and asked a second man, who responded, "Well, if I had a million dollars, I'd invest it in a chain of cheap, fast-food stores, and I'd make even more than a million dollars in profit right off." The wealthy man thought this was on the selfish side, and he looked further, stopping a logger to ask the same question. "What would I do with a million dollars? Well, I guess I'd just keep logging till it was all gone."[12]

Clearly this joke has a wide circulation. However, the Saskatchewan variant shows all the signs of how folklore becomes associated with a specific area. Rather than being a logger, fisherman, or some other occupation, the "hero" of the Saskatchewan version is naturally a farmer. Thus Robertson (or whoever originally brought the joke to the province) adapted the theme to a Saskatchewan setting. The style of presentation—a quick two-liner rather than an extended story—shows another kind of variation from the Oregon story. In addition, the joke has been adapted to modern times in Saskatchewan: rather than a millionaire, the source of wealth is the lottery, which is now very much a fact of life in this province.

Examples of any form of folklore might be used to explore the question of indigenous traditions. Indeed, simply discussing Saskatchewan folklore naturally raises and answers this question. The following three case studies are intended to expand upon some of the problems discussed so far. To call these case studies "representative" is a bit misleading since no one tradition can adequately represent the complexities of the folklore of almost one million people. However, these studies show a small part of what can be collected in the province, the breadth and variety of folklore in Saskatchewan. Perhaps most importantly, these case studies show that folklore is an everyday part of life in the province, that it is a vital activity in which everyone engages. These case studies reveal that creativity, in its various forms, abounds in Saskatchewan, and we need only open our eyes to discover the folklore around us.

3

An Evening
of Storytelling

Many stories are told during "special occasions"—parties, bed-times, verbal competitions. In other words, the telling of these tales must await those special circumstances when the teller is expected to perform, to please an avid and attentive audience of listeners. A bed-time story is a special end-of-day treat for children and eagerly awaited by them; the parent is as much aware of this eagerness as is the child, perhaps more so, and thus is put "on the spot" by the circumstances of telling a bed-time story. Similarly, in a joke-swapping or a competitive storytelling session in which the command, "now you tell one!" makes the teller the centre of attention, he becomes very conscious of his talents as a raconteur and is also very much "on the spot."

However, most storytelling occurs in more informal, relaxed settings. Chatting over a cup of tea, visiting friends for an evening of conversation, taking a break from work, passing the time while performing some boring or repetitive job, all lead to the kind of stories which are most common and most commonly told when people get together. What kind of stories are these? Although some of these informal tales might be jokes or purposeful lies, most are the recounting of everyday true events, recollections of happenings in the community, gossip about mutual acquaintances, stories of personal experiences, bits of history, and stories told as proof of a strongly-held conviction or as a testimony of belief.

Such tales, true and otherwise, are the basic element of casual conversation. Without these stories, conversations would become dry lectures made up of unsupported and abstract statements of belief and simple, unelaborated observations. No social occasion can sustain itself on such dry fare, and thus it is virtually impossible to carry on a conversation without telling stories. Even people who meet for the first time tell stories to one another, usually stories about themselves and their experiences.

Perhaps what is most valuable about these informal storytelling sessions is what can be learned about the people who engaged in them. For example, someone who has never flown in an airplane could learn much from eavesdropping on the casual storytelling conversation of air travellers. Similarly, one interested in learning about the everyday life and concerns of the people in Saskatchewan would be well-advised to sit around in a local store, a barbershop, or in a living room and listen to the stories that are told among the people in the community.

I recently had the pleasure of being part of just such an informal storytelling session at the home of a rancher, Carl Christensen, who has lived his entire life near Borden on the North Saskatchewan River. I had originally gone to Carl's home to collect tall tales from his long-time friend and neighbor, Wes Ingram, but the atmosphere was not right for the telling of tall tales. Indeed atmosphere, or context, is all-important in folklore, and that evening I learned a lesson about the proper context for the telling of tall tales. For these people, tall tales are reserved for the special atmosphere of the "corner store" (that is, the pub), picnic, or round-up, rather than for the living room, and I was told several times during the evening that the corner store was "the place for those kinds of stories."

Because I was in the context of an evening visit among neighbors, I would have to be satisfied with the types of stories that went along with this social occasion. Of course, I was more than satisfied: I was delighted with the stories which were told that night, for I learned more about Carl and Wes and their community than I would have during an entire evening of tall tales. Indeed, one tall tale was recounted by Carl, but under circumstances which made it fit well into the general flow of conversation; Carl told the tale in a special way, as will be discussed later.

Of course, the storytelling session which I observed was not quite the same as the usual evening's entertainment which these neighbors have enjoyed countless times before. The very fact that I was there—a stranger invited into the house to observe and record their conversation—affected the context considerably. Here is another lesson in collecting folklore: the observer always affects that which he observes. Thus, many of the stories were told especially for my benefit; that is, those in the living room tried hard to think of "good stories" that I might want to hear. In addition, when stories were told, details about local people and events that would have normally been left out of the account were included because of my ignorance of the history of the community. Thus, stories were continually being "footnoted" for my benefit. As well, I asked a number of naive and probing questions during the evening, which either altered the course of the natural conversational flow or forced the speakers to explain or expand on their subject in a way which would normally not have occurred if this evening were truly a "natural" get-together of neighbors.

However, bearing this artificiality in mind, the evening did progress in a relaxed fashion and was close enough to a natural evening of storytelling to show the kinds of tales which might normally occur during an evening's entertainment at the Christensens.

Let me set the scene. I entered the large and comfortable living room, where I was greeted by Carl and introduced to Wes and Elsie Ingram. Later, Carl's wife, Helga, joined the group, and the five of us made up the evening's gathering. However, talking was not the only activity going on. Helga crocheted during the evening, and at one point left the room to bring in coffee and cakes, which we all shared. A small dog belonging to the Christensens was also a part of the gathering and spent the entire evening going from one person to another seeking attention; thus, it was the shared responsibility of all in the room to spend some time petting the dog. But none of these activities interfered with conversation and were, rather, compliments to informal talk—crocheting, eating and drinking, petting the dog. In a sense, these activities made the atmosphere much more "natural" and much less like a folklore interview, which was all to the good.

In addition to these activities, we were joined at various times by children in the household. One or another of the children would unobtrusively come into the room and sit in part of the living room which might well be called the sidelines; that is, instead of intruding into the circle of five adults during the storytelling, the children stayed separate and became a transient group of observers of the scene. They had their own activities planned for that evening in other parts of the house, but during breaks to eat, or perhaps out of curiosity, they would leave off from their play or schoolwork to see what the adults were doing. What is particularly important about this activity is that it is through this means that the next generation picks up stories of community events and people. Consciously or unconsciously, the children were also "collecting" these tales, and undoubtedly they will be the bearers of these local traditions in later years when they become accepted into the informal conversation group of adults. The evolution is a natural one from child/observer to adult/participant in such situations, but the rules of etiquette and the boundaries of the "adult world" are still quite clearly defined. For example, at one point a young son of the Christensens came into the room to tell his mother something. He spoke in a whisper and was answered in a whisper by Helga and then was quickly shooed out of the room. He had entered the "adult circle" and he knew it. Thus, behind every informal get-together, there is a formal set of rules which are understood and obeyed by all. How to engage in conversation, what to talk about, how to behave towards a stranger, what stories are appropriate to the setting, who is permitted into the gathering, what activities are allowable or expected during conversation—rules govern all these situation and are quite noticeable to the observer, even if they are obeyed in an entirely unconscious manner.

But this informal conversation was also governed very much by the backgrounds and personalities of those present. I was a stranger who had come there expressly to collect stories, and I acted as the avid and interested outsider which I truly was. In this role, I generally remained silent, except to ask questions or show my agreement with what was being said. I was the "student", in effect, who was there to learn from my teachers—those who knew the traditions and stories of the area and who were capable of telling them to me. The others in the room, therefore, were active storytellers, although some were more active than others. However, all "took the floor" during the conversation when they felt that they had something special to communicate. But more about this later.

Although I had come expecting to hear stories from Wes Ingram, the main speaker of the evening was Carl, who was himself a storehouse of tales. Carl was born and raised in the community and is of Danish background. Now in his early forties, he has farmed and ranched in the same area as his immigrant father. His wife Helga is also an integral part of the farming and ranching operation, as came out quite clearly in the evening's conversation. She, however, is a relatively recent immigrant, having come over from Berlin, Germany, in 1961. Although fairly new to the area (by community standards), her interest in the community is great, and she has been active in compiling a local history of the area.

Wes and Elsie Ingram are a generation older than their neighbors. Wes was born in Alameda, near Estevan, and his family's roots, at least on his father's side, extend back far enough into Canadian history to be forgotten. His mother's family came over from England in 1886. He spent an adventurous and precarious life surviving the Depression and did not settle down in the Borden area until the late 1940s. Elsie was born in Birmingham, England, but she came to the Borden area as a very young child. She is of Quaker background and still practices the faith, as do a number of others in the area. Like their neighbors, the Ingrams are ranchers and farmers.

The different backgrounds of these four people meant that each had a certain specialized area when it came to storytelling. Carl was best on recounting local events, although he relied on Elsie and Wes for stories of events that happened before the 1940s. Both Wes and Elsie knew and could recount the older stories, but Wes less so, since his memories of the area do not extend back to childhood. However, Wes was a mine of Depression stories and memories of other parts of the country, although not very

49

many of these tales came up that evening. Helga, because of her interest in local history, knew many of the more noteworthy happenings in the community and could tell of them even though she did not experience these events herself. In addition, Helga the historian helped to jog the memories of the others and would "footnote" their tales with information which she has gathered in her collecting of local history. Of course, she was also a storehouse of tales pertaining to the life of an immigrant and that of a "green" farmwife—experiences which others in the room did not have.

Thus, when the conversation turned to a given subject, the one with the most "expertise" in that area would either tell a story, or be looked to by another teller for corroboration of details. In keeping with the relaxed nature of the evening, there was little movement or gesture during the storytelling, although Carl would at times move forward in his chair as he became more involved in his story, Wes would sometimes punctuate his conversation with his cane, and Helga's crocheting would markedly slow its pace when she was especially intent on getting a story across.

Before reading the account of the evening's conversation, be ready to make certain observations. Firstly, the stories speak very much of Saskatchewan culture and more specifically of the culture of the Borden area, for they reflect the concerns and perceptions of the people who tell them. The weather, animals, the landscape, agriculture, the ethnic mix, and community ethics and mores run through these stories as themes universally understood by people who live in rural Saskatchewan; collectively, these stories are a description of what it means to be a part of the Borden rural community. Secondly, note how the stories are told—how the tellers are creative and artistic in their accounts. Although most of the stories are of historical events and true experiences, there is still room for invention, for a clever turn of phrase, a slight exaggeration, an embellishment of a particular scene. In addition, the tellers show their adaptability by taking my ignorance into account; thus, their attention to detail is noticeable throughout the storytelling session. Thirdly, note the interplay of the four storytellers. While one is telling a story, the others encourage, corroborate and correct the account in progress. Quite often, two or more will collaborate in the telling of a tale, taking turns in the telling as the story unfolds, or one person will urge another to tell a certain story which they both know. The collaborative and cooperative effort present in this story-telling session indicates that we are dealing here with a shared tradition—a body of stories known by all members of the group, heard and told before, and perhaps understood on the same level by all members of the community. Of course, some stories are told better by one member of the group than by another and some of the stories were indeed new to one or more members of the group, but in general, these tales are a part of the local heritage of Borden and are as familiar to the people in that area as are the local landscape, the grid roads, the property boundaries, or the bends in the North Saskatchewan River.

The evening began with my unsuccessful attempt to elicit tall tales. Although no one felt able or willing to tell such stories, Wes did describe some contexts in which jokes and yarns would be more fitting:

Wes: *Oh generally at picnics or something like that.*
Elsie: *At round-ups, they used to—*
Wes: *Round-ups, anniversaries. See we used to run the community pasture up there, and we used to have a round-up every—at the beginning of June and then a round-up in the Fall. We used to round the cattle up in June to vaccinate the calves and castrate all the bull calves too. And we had a round-up again in the Fall when everybody came to get their cattle. And there used to be some real tall stories told up there. But God, I couldn't remember them now.*
Taft: *Well, that would be a general place for gathering then? Would it turn into a—*
Wes: *Oh yeah, the whole community would be there at that time.*[1]

Picnics, anniversary celebrations, and round-ups, but not evening visits: his point was well-made. But talk of tall tales did lead to the discussion of hunting stories, which often lend themselves to exaggeration or out-and-out lying. Thus, the first story of the evening was not a tall tale, but one in a similar vein—a recollection of true experiences surrounding a remarkable deer called Sluefoot.

Carl: *Oh we always used to watch the big bucks, and the neighbors would kind of keep an eye on them. There was one particular big buck that had one toe spread out to the side, and we called him Sluefoot. And he was around here for years and years and years. And a few guys saw him, but nobody ever, ever shot him that I know of. I had my chance at him.*

Wes: *He used to run right across our slough, right behind the hunters pretty near every year.*

Carl: *He might have been around for at least ten years.*

Wes: *Oh yeah, he was there for a long time. . . .*

Carl: *John Macpherson was a good hunter, an avid hunter. And John and I went out one day and caught him up near Eric's fence. And he turned and ran away, heading straight away from us. And we jumped out and lined up on him, and both shot directly right down this path that led into the fence. . . . And he was on that path and, by gosh, we couldn't figure out how we missed. But I think just when we shot, he must've turned to go up along the fence instead of going over it. And we walked down the path to see if we could see any blood, if we hit him. And the fence line was broken; the edges were just curled apart and splattered with lead. We broke the fence line just at the right height that he would have—*

Elsie: *You hit the fence?*

Carl: *Yeah, we hit the fence wire.*

Elsie: *Oh my.*

Carl: *And it broke the fence wire. Now, but there was no Sluefoot to be seen.*

Elsie: *Yeah, he just dodged in time.*

Carl: *Another time we were . . . about a quarter of a mile; we just saw him cut around the bush there. It's pretty open from there down to the feed lot, so we thought, well, all we'd have to do was come around Dick's old shack and we've got him dead to rights. So we drove around in the truck as fast as we could, and no sign of the deer anywhere. And we thought, well, there's probably a little bluff over here. He's probably in that little bluff. So we opened the gate and we drove over to that little bluff. And on the way over, we drove by a little patch of buckbrush. It was only about ten foot across and brush that high [one metre]. And we were heading for that bush, and as soon as we got fifty feet past that little patch of buckbrush, out comes this great big buck. He had just laid right down in the little patch of buckbrush and let us drive right by, and not five feet away.*

Elsie: *Oh my goodness.*

Carl: *It was right by the trail, and as soon as we were long gone, it headed in the other direction—*

Wes: *He was long gone the other way.*

Carl: *He was long gone the other way and took out like a bat out of heck over for section thirteen up here. We wheeled around and took off after him, but he was over the fence and into the bushes. We stopped at the road allowance, and—we used to pile all the rocks up against the fence on the property and then there'd be the fence line—and he took off. We could see his tracks where he had hunched in and dug his feet in for a jump. And he jumped over the rocks, over the fence, and he come landing on all fours skidding right in the centre of the road allowance. So in one leap, he made at least forty feet. That's the kind of buck he was.*

Wes: *Oh yes, he was—*

Carl: *—tremendously smart. And he could hide in the littlest patch of brush. And we had a lot of fun just trying to get close to him.*

From deer-hunting, the conversation naturally turned to goose and duck hunting, and then took a more general turn to a discussion of the current return of large flocks of geese to the area after years of little or no fowl. Just as hunting tales often become exaggerated into tall tales, any story of "plentitude" is likely to be embellished in order to accentuate the point of the story. Thus, in this tale of the great number of geese on Carl's property, our belief was tested by an account which has many of the elements of a tall tale. Yet, Carl tells the tale as a true, personal experience:

Carl: *But in just the past few years, we've had geese come back, and a lot of them. And it was such an unusual occurrence. It was a few years ago, three or four years ago, we had a wet Fall. And I had a field of barley out. And the geese came in there to land every night and they'd go down to the* river and spend the night on an island. Then they'd come up in the morning and evening to feed on the barley. And we didn't say too much; we didn't want them scared away because the kids would go out and wait for the school bus and just loved to watch the geese coming in, and they could hear them coming. And so when it dried up, I went out and was combining that barley. It was at night, and all of the sudden I got down to the end and the combine ran so quiet that I thought that there was a chain gone off, or something like that, or maybe something plugged up. There was just no noise. So I reached around and stuck my hand back into where the grain comes into the hopper and was driving a long way until I got something in my hand, and pulled it around and hung it in front of the light, and took a look at what I had got out of the bin. And it was nothing but goose manure. They'd eaten all of the barley out of that spot. And of course there was no rattle of grain through the cylinder, and that was why it was running so quiet. And as I said, all I got in my hand was goose manure.

Helga: That's not what you usually call it!

The conversation then drifted back to deer from geese, and Wes told a story of smart deer before the conversation turned away from wildlife to other topics:

Wes: I know that they used to come and hunt on our land for deer, and now we got it posted [for no hunting]. Two years ago, Johnny Macpherson came down there and he finally drove down and he wanted to know if he could shoot a deer on our place, because there was seven deer standing right across the fence from Ens's. And Johnny said they were there every morning. They were on our side of the fence. They never come over on that side of the fence. So they know where they're safe.

The mention of Wes's property in the above story prompted Carl to talk about the history of Wes's ranch and how it was one of the earliest in the area. The conversation then naturally turned to a discussion of the history of ranching in the region and of the large cattle drives of the last century. In relation to these drives, Helga asked Wes when he came to the area as a cowboy, and then the discussion shifted to a brief history of Wes's life. Out of the history of places where Wes had worked came an anecdote which Carl brought to Wes's mind:

Carl: *Isn't that the place where there were all the Walners? A bunch of Joe Walners?*
Wes: *There was thirty-two Joe Walners on the mail route there. I wasn't on the mail route, but I used to meet the mailman every morning. [. . .]*
Taft: *That must have been a tough route to deliver mail. How did he know when—*
Wes: *He said if there was no initials on it, he just threw so much in each box. I asked him that very question. I said, "How do you tell?" And that's what he told me. He said, "I just put a bunch in each box."*

This humorous anecdote led to a number of others, again all true, as we turned from "unusual but true" stories to "funny but true" tales. What followed were several stories about local characters. Indeed the local character is a universal subject of tales: the crazy, the eccentric, the stupid, the clever, the volatile, the meek, the very rich, the very poor—anyone who is different from the norm is likely to become the butt of stories and jokes within the community. For example, Carl recalled the following personal experience about his visit with an old bachelor:

Carl: *But there was an old bachelor over here. When we were kids growing up here, we were about the only really young kids in the area. We were surrounded by older folks. And most of them didn't have children. And they were all uncles and aunts to us. And this old Norwegian bachelor that lived over there by himself, he wasn't the world's greatest housekeeper by any stretch of the imagination. I remember going over there one time with another kid hunting crow's eggs. And of course in those days nobody saw anybody too often, so when anybody did arrive, you had to put out the big welcome. And you had to come in and have a cup of coffee. So this old bachelor welcomed us in there just like grown-up adults, you see. . . . His coffeepot, like I said, it was huge and it was filled to within an inch of the top with old coffee grounds. And he reached his gnarled knuckles into a bag of coffee and pulled out a little pinch of coffee and added that to the top, and then filled it up with water for whatever this pot would hold. And kind of a muddy concoction came out and that was "coffee." And I can remember, he asked us if we wanted sugar, and we did. And he got the sugar bowl, and the sugar bowl looked as though it was finished in some kind of suede. But it wasn't suede—it was a kind of mixture of grime and fly specks on the outside of it. It made it look like a kind of suede leather. And I can remember my horror: he chewed snuff, and he'd just turn around from the table and spit on the floor. To me, I had never seen anything like that in my life. And then, of course, he'd take this snuff box and tap the lid and crank it open and pass it around. And of course we, by that time, believed that we were pretty big fellows, so we tried this snuff. And the kid I was with, in a second or two, ran for the door and got rid of it. But I—my dad chewed snuff—so I knew how you were supposed to handle it. So I kind of let my tongue wad it into my cheek. But not wanting to spit, because spitting was—*

Wes: *Forbidden.*

Carl: *I was taught that it was not right. The saliva just kept building and building and I didn't know what to do with it, so I swallowed it.*

Elsie: *Oh dear.*

Carl: *All of the sudden the room got dark, and I woke up on the old bachelor's bed. I had passed right out. So that was the first and the last snuff I ever had. That's for sure.*

Although such a tale is told for its humour, it also teaches us much about what was considered socially acceptable. We learn of some of the rules of hospitality on the prairie, some of the differences, as seen by a young boy, between normal family life and the life of an old loner. The very fact that this old bachelor is pointed out as a "character" and that he is a worthy subject of such a story tells us something about the place of single men in a rural Saskatchewan community.

If bachelordom led to gossip and stories, so did drunkenness. Carl and Wes followed the bachelor tale with stories of two other local characters: Nick and Katie, who were the major suppliers of moonshine for the area, but who also seemed to be their own best customers:

Wes: *Well they're another story again. I mean Nick and Katie.*
Carl: *Where did they come from originally?*
Elsie: *Romania.*
Carl: *Was it Romania?*
Elsie: *Yes.*
Carl: *And Nick always had a batch of brew going. And sometimes as kids we'd have to go and find a lost horse—a horse that had wandered away. And we'd roam the countryside. And I can remember, I was maybe ten or eleven—my brother was about five years younger, so that would make him maybe six or seven—and we got down in that country. And when we got to the house, we noticed that Nick was asleep on the sofa, and his wife was in a great state of animation which we didn't know anything about. And apparently they had got into the mash a little too soon, and he got kind of indisposed and she was fairly high. And there was nothing doing, but this cute little boy, which was my younger brother, had to be hugged and kissed to no end, much to his embarrassment. And he still remembers that to this day.*
Wes: *I'll tell you another time. Harry and I were going up to pasture. We used to ride that way on horseback all the time. And I guess they'd been into the mash pretty heavy that day because Katie come out and she done her darnedest to get on horseback with Harry for a long time, and she tried to get on horseback with me first. Over half a mile, she kept coming. We had a heck of a time [escaping her].*

After some discussion of illicit home brew in the area, I intruded into the natural flow of the conversation to ask about social occasions when storytelling, singing and dancing might occur. Thereupon the topic became community dances, box socials, whist drives, Christmas visits, and picnics, as well as a discussion of those who attended, played musical instruments or sang. At one point Wes protested that he knew less than others about such matters because he only settled in this area thirty years ago; Elsie and Carl were better sources on community socials. Following the idea of social gatherings, I then asked if people gathered in town very often. Elsie responded that the farmers rarely went to town except for business purposes. Carl added that Langham, rather than Borden, was the place people went to in the winter since a trip across the frozen river cut the distance to Langham by many miles.

With the mention of wintertime, the conversation turned to one of the most common topics among farmers and ranchers—the weather. As Wes pointed out, "Yes, the weather is about the first thing you'd say when you meet your neighbor." Thus, there followed a number of stories about harsh weather, especially blizzards. Like hunting, the weather is a natural subject for exaggeration and tall tales, and once again the credibility of the group was tested by a "strange but true" tale told by Carl:

Carl: *But you know I think it was in the late forties or early fifties, the snow that we had here was just, oh, tremendous.*
Elsie: *I tell you what. Tell him [Taft] about the blizzard. [...]*
Taft: *Yeah, go ahead.*
Wes: *That's the one that Carl was leading up to.*
Carl: *Some of the blizzards and some of the storms—we didn't have field shelter-belts—and so when the storms came up, you got blowing snow that just drifted in around the yards and piled up sometimes to where, when we were kids walking on the snowdrifts, we could step right over the telephone lines. Because there'd be a quarter section pretty well clear, and then the bush around the yard. And it would just pile up there. And I think Wes can tell you all kinds of stories about hauling hay in that kind of—*
Wes: *Yeah I was hauling straw from Carl's dad here one winter, and I was driving right over top of the telephone wires with a team and sleigh.*
Helga: *Aw!*
Wes: *That's—*
Carl: *Yes!*
Wes: *That's God's truth. Right down here about a mile—*
Helga [to Taft]: *Besides it doesn't matter if this is truth or fiction.*

58

Wes: *Well that was the truth.*

Elsie: *I know. You've told me. But it [the wires] was fairly low, I guess.*

Wes: *Because I was hauling right up—I was coming straight up from the gate.*

Carl: *Yeah.*

Wes: *And I was coming back one day and the neighbor come along and told me that I couldn't drive across his land hauling straw. So I come up around the next turn, and I come right over the top of the telephone wires. That's a fact. But another time we had a snowstorm, a blizzard. Carl had just got a truck at that time, and he went to town with a load of grain. Didn't you? To Borden?*

Here another story began, but it is important to look back at the previous tale to see the struggle between truth and fiction which marks any storytelling session. Helga was sceptical about the height of the snowdrifts as reported by Carl and Wes. To her, their story was dangerously close to being a tall tale. It was now up to Wes, Carl, and Elsie to "back up" their belief in the height of the snowdrifts. Wes became quite emphatic in attesting to the truth of the story. Elsie tried to moderate by lowering the height of the telephone poles, making the snowdrifts more believable for Helga. Carl, perhaps anticipating Helga's or my disbelief, prefaced the story with an explanation of the lack of snow barriers in past times. In addition to these tactics, Wes brought in more detail about exactly why and where he hauled the straw in order to make his story appear more historical and factual. Whether they persuaded Helga of the truth of the story is an open question, but the more important point is that all four were intent on maintaining the context which they had established at the beginning of the evening—a time for true stories.

Perhaps because of Helga's scepticism, the remaining blizzard stories were not of the "strange but true" variety: rather, they were stories of near tragedy in which either they or people they knew came close to perishing in the cold and snow. Some of the tales were humorous in intent; for example, Carl's tale of how he once refused to borrow a pair of skis from Wes for the trek home, and how he had to struggle through hip-deep snow without any skis. He surely would have frozen to death if it wasn't for the fact that he was a young man at the time and, in Wes's words, "full of vinegar." Other tales, such as the following, told of serious events in which lives were truly at stake:

Elsie: *But I was thinking of the time the kids never got home from school. . .*

Wes: *Well that wasn't so long ago.*

Elsie: *They only had a mile and a half to go.*

Wes: *That was in '55, wasn't it?*

Carl: *Wasn't long ago! It was only about thirty years ago!*

Wes: *What?*

Carl: *It was only about thirty years ago! . . .*

Wes: *'55, wasn't it?*

Taft: *What happened then?*

Carl: *There was a big blizzard come up.*

Wes: *It was a beautiful day to start out with.*

Carl: *Oh, a tremendous day.*

Elsie: *It started out a very mild day.*

Wes: *It was raining.*

Carl: *And then—I know there was no snow. I drove the truck; took Ritchie to school. And then there was a weather warning come out, and the teacher said, "OK, we'll shut down the school at noon, and send the kids home." All the kids went home except the Panner kids. And they only lived two miles from school.*

Wes: *Mile and a half, really.*

Elsie: *And they couldn't ride across country for as long as that?*

Carl: *No.*

Wes: *Well, it would be two miles, yeah.*

Carl: *Nearly two miles. And so by the time they left the school, it had come up pretty good. And they got about half way—*

Wes: *They got about half way across the field, yeah—*

Carl: *I think that's as far as they got.*

Wes: *Yeah.*

Elsie: *The truck stopped.*

Wes: *The truck stopped. So he [the children's father] went home. He left the kids in the truck and he went home to get a tractor. And he got back about three quarters of a mile—just by the Dean house, a little over half a mile. And he couldn't get any further with the tractor. That's how much snow had come in that short a time. So he walked back over to where the kids were, and told them he was going home to—*

Elsie: *Joshua come back with him, and he stayed with the children, yeah.*

Wes: *Oh, Joshua come back with him on the tractor. And then he went home again and he heated up some stones. Why they didn't carry the kids home, I'll never know. Or why they didn't make them walk.*

Elsie: *Well, there was a terrible wind. It was awful.*

Wes: *Oh yeah, it was terrific. But anyhow John [the father] went down and he got lost. And he ended up in that bush at Duncan Macpherson's corner.*

Elsie: *And he built a fire in the middle—*

Wes: *And he built a fire in the bush, and he stayed there all night.*

Carl: *And the kids were in the truck all night.*

Wes: *And the kids were in the truck with Joshua all night.*

Taft: *And they were OK?*

Wes: *Yeah, they were OK.*

Elsie: *Well they were, but their dad said the hardest thing he ever did was to open the door in the morning. He thought he'd find them all frozen. But Joshua just kept them rubbing their legs and keeping their feet warm.*

Wes: *Yeah.*

Elsie: *And singing to them.*

But whether the stories of blizzards were humorous or serious, their point was the same: in this part of the country, the weather is unpredictable and dangerous, and one must respect and be prepared for the harsh conditions of the winter.

From cold winters the conversation drifted to the topic of hot summers; then to the discussion of droughts, bad crop years, the effects of the Great Depression, and dust storms. Wes was the expert on the Depression, and he told stories of the miserable harvests of the thirties. At this point, I forced a change in the topic by asking Wes a bit more about his background, about where his parents settled, and when he was born. In short order, I elicited the family histories of Carl and Elsie. A discussion of the specific ethnic backgrounds of those in the room naturally led to talk of the many different ethnic groups in the area. From this, the conversation drifted on to the struggle of farmers in the area to pay their taxes, and all agreed that the farmers here were always prompt in their payments, for to fall behind led quickly to failure.

However, it occurred to Helga that a certain group of people in the area were not known for their hard work or reliability, and she reminded the rest of the group of the squatters in the hills by the river. These squatters were known as Forty-One Seveners, named after the township and range numbers where they lived. Some inhabited the shacks of farmers who had abandoned the poor land near the river, and some even lived in caves on the river bank:

Helga: *But those people, those squatters, how many were there? Because mom [her mother-in-law] told me that she went with the doctor there to deliver babies. And she said she remembers this dreadful [place]. Oh, and she didn't know where to put this new-born baby. Because everything was so terribly filthy. And it was dripping through—it was raining.*
Carl: *Chickens were on the bed, under the bed.*
Helga: *Yeah.*
Carl: *Fluffing their feathers in the dirt under the bed while the baby was being born.*
Elsie: *Well, that was one of the—*
Wes: *Forty-One Seveners.*
Helga: *Yeah.*
Carl: *Yeah.*
Helga: *But how many lived there? I mean five, six, twenty?*
Carl: *And then it rained—*
Wes: *How many families?*
Helga: *Yeah.*
Wes: *Oh, there was I don't know how many families. There must have been thirty-five or forty families up there.*
Helga: *Is that right?*
Taft: *Gee.*
Elsie: *Through the year, at one time.*

Carl: *The sod, the sod on this particular building. When they came [the doctor and his mother], shortly after they arrived, they got a thunderstorm, and it started dripping through the roof. And the mud—the dirt floor turned to mud. And the doctor got... disgusted with kind of wading in the mud on the floor, so he went out to the outside. Grabbed one of the boards that was half off the side of the house. Ripped it off and laid it across the floor to walk on.*
Wes: *Yeah, there were some pretty rough places up there.*

The stories continued, ending with a description of how a local reeve lured these squatters into Saskatoon with the promise of jobs and then burned down their shacks when they had left. I again forced a change in the conversation by asking Helga about her background. She ended her brief life history by stressing that she was very interested in local history and had helped to put together a history book about the area. I then asked if the people talked much about the history of the region, and this led to more stories, especially about those events which "don't make the history books."

Helga recalled stories from Carl's uncle who was a policeman in Borden and who, quite naturally, knew of all the crimes and shady dealings in the area. As Helga and the others were quick to point out, however, this kind of gossip about illegal activities is a part of the heritage of any small town—no place is without its seamy side. To prove her point, Helga described another district she had heard of which was branded "Little Chicago" because of the general lawlessness of its population. Gossip concerning criminal activities is indeed to be found in every community, and the widespread fascination with illegality and immorality is quite understandable. The unusual, the abnormal, the uncharacteristic behaviour of people is the essence of stories. Sometimes this behaviour grows out of unusual situations as in the tales of how people act during a blizzard. But at other times, this behaviour is seen by the tellers as stemming from the personality or background of an individual, or indeed as arising out of the common traits, whether ethnic, religious, or social, of an entire group.

Local character stories, as discussed earlier, certainly fall under the category of tales about unusual behaviour, and thus it is not surprising that the conversation soon turned again to this topic. The Borden area, like so many other communities in Saskatchewan, once played host to remittance men—those poor souls who had come from well-off British families and who, for lack of any training or ambition, were sent packing to Canada. Those who usually became the butt of stories were the ones who could not adapt to the new land, the ones who knew nothing about farming and ranching and had not acquired any of the skills that would allow them to live and prosper on the prairies. Elsie recalls one such man:

Elsie: *I knew only one.*
Carl: *Who was that?*
Elsie: *Leslie Baker.*
Helga: *Yeah.*
Carl: *That's before my time. You'll have to tell that, Elsie.*
Elsie: *Well he was a queer duck. He was an old bachelor and he lived alone. And one winter he got lost. And so instead of wandering around, he tied himself to a tree or post, and went round it and round it, and said, "Lost on the prairie. Lost on the prairie." And it just happened that he wasn't very far from a shack with people in it. And they heard this guy going round saying, "Lost on the prairie." They went and rescued him. But he probably would have frozen to death. He was cold.*
Helga: *Didn't he live near Maggie McShean? That isn't where he was saved?*
Elsie: *He lived around Baxter's place. Somewhere there.*
Helga: *Well, there's a lady . . . and she was talking about him. And that he always had a box of candy sitting on the shelf for the ladies when they came.*
Elsie: *Oh, he was very polite.*
Helga: *And I think Maggie had a little crush on him. It sort of seemed to come through.*
Elsie: *Did she?*
Helga: *I guess by the sound of it, he came from a very well-to-do family. And therefore his manners and his way of dressing—*
Elsie: *He was quite refined, yeah. . . . He used to go around. He'd dig post holes for people—corner posts. He'd*

take three days over one, but he made a beautiful job. He was very particular. But of course you kept him and he had his meals.

Helga: *That's one way of getting your feed.*

The discussion continued on remittance men and what became of them. If these men were unsuccessful at farming and could not contribute to the community in any material way, they nevertheless made their contribution as the source of many local character stories.

The fact that stories of local crime and tales of the less reputable or less successful members of the community were never reported in the local histories was on the minds of everyone in the room at this point. Seeing the tape recorder made Wes wish that some of the old-timers in the community had been taped while they were alive. A pensive mood momentarily hung over the group, until I broached a new subject by asking Carl about an anniversary poem that he had written for the Ingrams. Helga noted that such poems run in Carl's family and that his mother is well known as a local poet. Some of her poems are satirical and make fun of family members and friends. To illustrate what she meant, Helga told a story on herself:

Helga: *I tell you, it's in the family, though. His mother made up a poem for some [bridal] shower once. You remember that one, don't you?*

Wes: *Yeah, she can make them up, too.*

Helga: *Yes. And I was, of course, green as grass and didn't know how to cook, bake or anything else. And quite rightly, when my first batch of bread came along, it was a pretty lousy effort—and disappeared. But somehow mom got wind of that one. And then we had to go to the shower of a friend. And here she made up this poem. And I said, "Oh, make me up one. I don't know how to make up poems." So she says, "Well, OK." And I had to read it, and it was about my bread not going right and beautifully. And I wanted to hide it and, no, if I hid it, the dog would dig it up. So finally I chucked it in the dug-out. So goes the story. And then here, as we saw the next day, driving past the dug-out, there is this fantastic thing floating on the dug-out. Looks like a flying saucer or*

*something like this, you know. And having, or course, been
greatly surprised, and my being very, very embarrassed. And
she put it in beautiful [verse]. I'm afraid I can't lay my hands
on it [the poem]. But it was a masterpiece. And that was, of
course, my masterpiece, you know, that I didn't admit to.
Anyway, then he [Carl] was really quite a darling, and sort of
ignored this strange apparition on the dug-out. But the worst
thing that hurt my feelings terribly—all my friends thought
it was true!*

Such a tale is yet another type of story common in
informal conversations: the personal experience story told at
the expense of the teller. Just as stories about foolish local
characters are a part of storytelling sessions, personal foolish
tales abound. They are the equivalent of the joke, but the fool
is the one telling the tale. Unlike the local character story,
however, this type of tale requires that the teller sacrifice
some of her dignity before the group. Yet the person who is
unable to tell a fool tale on himself is perhaps the one who
sacrifices the most, for the ability to laugh at oneself is a
necessary ingredient for an attractive personality in our
culture. Such tales are interesting from a social point of view,
for in certain situations one can tell a fool tale at another's
expense. A very close friend or a loved-one can get away with
such a breach of etiquette, if everyone in the storytelling
session is aware of the teller's true feelings towards the butt of
the joke. In other words, only a true friend can insult you and
get away with it.

For example, immediately following Helga's tale, Elsie
recalled a similar story about her mother-in-law. Even if Carl
or Helga knew the story, it was only Elsie or Wes who could
tell it without breaking the rules of story etiquette:

Elsie: *Well, grandma used to tell this about the bread that
wouldn't rise. You know, and she couldn't get it to rise. And
she kept it a day or two and it didn't rise. So she was like you
[Helga]. She didn't want her husband to know about it. It
was very serious. So she went and buried it in the garden.*
Wes: *This was my mother.*
Elsie: *Yeah. And after a while—*
Wes: *When she first got married.*

66

Elsie: —*it started to rise and it rose up dirt and all. So she couldn't hide it any longer.*

The two personal fool tales remind Helga of other storytelling contexts in which fanciful jokes and tall tales were appropriate: "I'd say that if you want to hear some tall stories, I should imagine that you stop off occasionally at the corner shops." I replied by asking if good stories were told at the corner store in Borden, and all agreed that they were. Carl then felt the need to give an example of a "corner store" story for my benefit. Here we have a most peculiar situation: although the context was not right for the telling of tall tales, Carl was able to tell one nevertheless without breaking the rules of the evening. Before discussing how he managed to fit a tall tale into a true-story session, let us look at his tale:

Carl: *I remember one time when it had rained. And somebody had stopped in off the highway, and was kind of saying how much it had rained and how bad the mud was and all this. And I don't know whether he was making this one up or whether he was repeating one that he had heard, but anyway it was new to us. He said that the mud that we had here was nothing. He'd come in with a semi and pulled in to old Dick Byzorko's bulk station and buried that semi.*
Wes: *Uh-huh, yeah.*
Carl: *And then of course to drown his sorrows at having this semi just absolutely buried right up to the flat deck in mud, he went down to the corner store. And happened along. And of course he was entertaining, and being the brunt of jokes about his semi. And he said, well the mud we had here was nothing compared to the mud they had back up in his country, in heavy clay country, when he was a kid. And he said that when the drought came to an end there, it started raining and it rained for three days straight. And after the rain had quit, they found that their pigs had got out. And so they went to hunt these pigs. And the pigs had taken off down the road and they followed the tracks. And after a few hours, they caught up to the pigs. They were all dead. And of course we fell for it: "Well, what happened?" "Well," he said, "when they got going down the road, the mud would just cling to anything. It would just build up. A car going*

down the road would build up mud on the wheels until it
couldn't clear the fenders, and it would just stall the engine."
He said, "These pigs got going down the road, and it was
muddy, and the mud started to build up on their tails. And it
got bigger and bigger and bigger on their tails, and it
stretched the skin over their backs so tight, they couldn't
close their eyes. And they all died for lack of sleep."[2]

Carl was able to tell this story that evening because he
was in fact telling a true story about the telling of a tall tale.
In other words, by telling the tall tale "once removed," he
was describing the actual situation in which such stories are
told; that is, he was giving a true account of a tall-tale-telling
session. For this reason, he gave a long preface to the story
itself in which he set up the scene as he remembered it in the
pub that day. The technique of "the story within the story" is
an old literary device, but it also serves as a way of
introducing a tale which would ordinarily be out of place.

The telling of this tall tale prompted Helga to ask me
about folklore and what a folklorist collects. She commented
that there was much folklore in Europe, but that she
wondered about the extent of traditions in such a new land as
Saskatchewan. In response to Helga's statement, the others
began talking of Indian remains and artifacts in the area—
the oldest historical traditions in the community. There
followed talk of arrowheads, teepee rings, and buffalo bones
found by one or another member of the community over the
years. They alluded to stories of fur traders' routes that went
through the community and to Gabriel Dumont's passage
through the area. Wes recalled that an old Metis man who
came through the area had told stories of finding gold in the
river mud, but no one ever followed up on the old man's
claims.

As if the group were following an unconscious
chronology, they gradually shifted the conversation away
from ancient history to nineteenth-century history and then
to more contemporary events. As if to end the historical
sketch of the Borden area, Elsie, Helga, and Carl told stories
about John Diefenbaker, which again "never made the
history books":

Elsie: *Of course you'll find references around Halcyonia that John Diefenbaker went to [i.e., taught] school there.*

Wes: *Yeah.*

Elsie: *What you don't find in the history books, though, is the fact that John Diefenbaker got thrown out because he played hookey with the boys when the school inspector came.*

Helga: *Did he?*

Carl: *The inspector came. He got fired because he went out with the kids to snare gopher tails when he was supposed to have school.*

Helga: *And when he was, in his memoirs, saying how the mounties used to stop in at their shack here where their homestead is, that they gave them hospitality. There was a former neighbor of his living out in B.C. who did not belong to the same party as John Diefenbaker. And he just snorted and said, "Humph, the place wasn't even big enough for members of the family, let along anybody else going there to stay."*

Carl: *"There was hardly room enough to swing a cat," if you want to know how he put it.*[3]

Elsie, however, does recall the mounties stopping in at homesteads for meals.

At this point there was a lull in the conversation although the history of the area was still on our minds. Helga picked up the discussion again by saying how amazed she was, when she first came to this country, that one could still find and speak to the first settlers of the land. Her point was that in listening to the stories of the settlers, most seemed to be accounts of good people and good times. But as a counter-example, she recalled a story of a particularly mean man. Thus, the conversation returned to talk of a local character:

Helga: *Now and then there's a little story popping up. Like that guy at Eagle Creek who was the meanest whatever-you-want-to-call-it guy there ever was. I guess around that country they had stories galore. How mean he was to people. "One of these days, he's going to get it." And somebody kills him. The guy disappeared, right? So everybody swore blind, somebody did him in. Buried him in the bush some place by the river. Nobody found it.*

Carl: *Oh yeah. Well in fact a relative of mine in Edmonton had heard the story that this guy had been done in. And the guy told him, he says, "I can show you the spot where he's buried." And my uncle told me, "But don't say anything about this. I don't want to get involved in anything like that." "Heck no, I won't say anything." "But anyway, I was told on good authority that this guy just disappeared one dark night, and this guy told me that he could show me the spot where he was buried." Well, two or three years later, the guy's daughter died. And here he turns up from I-don't-know-where for the funeral. So it must have been a little bit of—*

Elsie: *Oh, this is Mike you're talking about.*

Carl: *Yeah, this is Mike.*

Wes: *Yeah, we heard that he was—*

Elsie: *—been done in.*

Wes: *Yup.*

Helga: *I thought, gee what a country, you know.*

Carl: *Oh yeah. And I heard via Edmonton. Not through here at all, that he'd been done in. Yeah.*

From unusual individuals, the conversation immediately turned to unusual groups, specifically the Doukhobors. There followed a number of stories of some of the more radical demonstrations put on by this group in past years. And once again the conversation turned from unusual groups to unusual activities: mention of a place where Doukhobors held a demonstration brought to Carl's mind the fact that the same area had one of the largest illicit stills in the community. Thus, the conversation made its way back to the topic of whiskey and moonshine. The following story is a natural outgrowth of the conversational drift:

Carl: *But one of the great mysteries of course that they ever had in Borden was a carload of whiskey was shunted on to a siding there one weekend. And when they picked it back up again, the car was empty.*

Elsie: *Was empty.*

Carl: *A whole carload of whiskey disappeared—*

Wes: *—disappeared—*

70

Carl: —*over a weekend. And they brought Pinkerton detectives in from the States and had railroad cops all over the place. They interviewed living-in-town people. They searched the sand hills south of town.*

Elsie: *Did they?*

Carl: *Uh-huh. And they went on for a number of years hunting up leads and all the rest of it to this carload of whiskey that disappeared. But never, ever—*

Wes: —*found a bottle.*

Carl: —*found hide nor hair of a trace or even a whisper of what might have happened to it. But a whole carload of whiskey disappeared.*

Without stopping for breath, Carl launched into another story which was obviously related to the previous one as far as the subject of whiskey was concerned. However, the next story represents yet another kind of tale acceptable in a true-tale-telling session. Just as there are stories about foolish people and foolish acts, there are many stories about cleverness. The following story is clearly a "clever trickster" tale, and in theme if not in content it is a part of an age-old tradition of such tales found in many different cultures. From the trickster Raven found in Indian tales to the clever student of medieval European stories, this theme has never lost its popularity. Today, the clever trickster appears in the popular media in such guises as Bugs Bunny or as the private detective who outwits the villain (and the police) through cleverness and deception.

Following the taletelling rules of the evening, if a clever trickster tale was to be told, it must be one of a true clever incident. Thus, Carl's next story not only continues the topic of whiskey and the stealing of whiskey, but it also introduces a new kind of true tale into the evening's entertainment:

Carl: *A real good friend of dad's was a station agent. And he used to have whiskey dropped off there before prohibition for the hotel.*

Wes: *Oh yeah.*

Carl: *In big barrels, big casks. And dad was over to the agent's. And the agent [was] in this little locked room that they had there . . . between the telegraph and where they used*

71

to park the cream cans. There was this locked room?

Wes: *Uh-huh, yeah.*

Carl: *And took him through there, and there was this big barrel of whiskey standing there. And he [the agent] said, "Boy, I've got to guard that. They won't be picking it up till tomorrow morning. And I better watch that nobody gets at it." Kind of joking, dad said, "Well," he says, "I'm going to steal it on you tonight." And he [the agent] said, "No you won't, because I'm going to watch it." Dad said, "Oh, I'm going to get it." Dad kind of looked at it: the station platform was later filled in, but it was about two and a half feet up in the air, and it was later all filled in with cinders and gravel and everything else. And dad had sized up the room, and being a blacksmith all his life, he could, with his eye, measure things. And he went back to his shop after dark, [returned], and crawled under the platform and drilled with a drill up through the floor. And drilled into the keg of whiskey.*

Elsie: *Oh, and drained it?*

Carl: *Yeah, shoved a piece of tubing in there and drained the keg right where it stood. And the next morning, the guy came for his barrel.*

Wes: *There was no whiskey.*

Carl: *He had emptied it. Yeah, dad did that.*

Elsie: *Why did he do it?*

Carl: *Because the guy said he couldn't do it. That was the only reason. He said that no way that dad could steal it, and dad told him he was going to steal it. And so he crawled under the platform and drilled up through it and drained the keg right where it stood. Yeah.*

Elsie: *What did he do with the whiskey? Drink it?*

Carl: *Oh, I don't know.*

Wes: *Let it go on the ground.*

Helga: *I don't believe it.*

Carl: *I don't believe so. I think he was much too frugal for that.*

Helga: *He was a typical Dane, don't forget.*

Carl: *Yes.*

In keeping with many clever trickster tales, the hero performs his deed, not for personal gain, but for the challenge and joy of outwitting the dupe.

Helga's concluding statement to the above story, "He was a typical Dane, don't forget," led to a kind of ethnic-joke bantering between Helga and Carl. My impression was that this couple engaged in this type of verbal play—Dane against German—as a form of mild "friendly insulting" discussed earlier, and that this banter occurred quite frequently when they joked between themselves. As if to confirm my impression, the Christensens expanded their bantering into the following stories. In each case the teller relates a personal experience story in which he or she gets the better of the other through a timely quip. These stories, then, are further examples of the kind of joke or fool tale which a person is allowed to tell about a loved-one.

These stories also fall into the category of clever trickster tales. However, in each case the teller is the trickster, and the trick consists of a witticism or retort. The following stories are very similar in structure to each other in that most of the tale involves the detailed setting up of a final scene in which the clever quip is used. In addition, these stories seem to start off as serious tales in which injury to the "dupe" almost occurs. After hearing Carl's tale, Helga's seemed such a natural rejoinder that I wondered if they were paired often in storytelling sessions. Carl's opening statement follows directly after Helga's concluding remark about Danes and leads from the introductory bantering to his true-story joke told at the expense of his wife:

Carl: *She comes from Germany and in Germany they always say that Danes are careful. And I always—*
Helga: *There are a lot of them around here that are.*
Carl: *And anyway—*
Helga: *Like you.*
Carl: *I always like to tell the story: when I was combining. When I was combining after a long period of rain, and I was going to try a field of oats. And so I went out and took a sample and gave it to Helga and said, "Now you hustle your butt and get that tested. Because if it's fit, I want to go." She went to town and on the way back—she had to take the [oat]*

test—on the way back from town, she was hot-footing it a little too fast. She hit a patch of loose gravel and the car started swerving back and forth across the road. And just then the school bus came around the curve. She said, "Oh my gosh, if I keep this up, I'm going to hit the school bus. But there's a big field and a shallow ditch, and I'll just let it go off into the ditch and off to the field. And that way I won't hit the bus." And there was weeds about this high on the edge of the ditch—they hadn't mowed the ditch—and she just took the ditch and be-damned if she didn't hit the approach. And the car hit the approach and went way up in the air and came crashing down on the approach and just broke the back of the car. Fortunately, she wasn't hurt. She had a box of blue grapes—you know these baskets of blue grapes with a little gauze cover?

Taft: *Yeah.*

Carl: *In the back of the car—when I went to pick up the car later, there was not one single grape on the stem. There was individual grapes all over the car, but there was not—because I looked for it—there was not one single grape on the stem.*

Helga: *And the car reeked of grapes.*

Carl: *Yes. But anyway, I came from the combine into the house to get a manual out and the tachometer to check the fan speed. Just then the phone rang. It's Helga in a very, very timorous voice, and shook up a bit. She said, "I uh, I uh, I hit the ditch and I wrecked the car." I said, "Well,"—and [she was] kind of wanting sympathy, I could hear—and—*

Helga: *I needed it.*

Carl: *I said, "Did anybody get hurt?" "No, no, no one got hurt." I said, "How did the oats test?" And she's never forgiven me for that.*

As a joke on Helga, this tale is interesting in several respects. As becomes quite apparent in Helga's rebuttal, part of the joke of the tale is Helga's lack of control of the car. The importance in the agricultural world of being in complete control of cars, trucks, tractors, combines, and other large and complex machinery cannot be overstressed. Thus, part of the joke on Helga is her loss of control; compare Carl's description of how his wife controlled the car with his account of his careful and considered approach to the combine. The comparison is clear.

This comparison of his wife's lack of control with his own control is then transferred from machinery to speech. Carl mimics his wife's frantic, uncontrolled account of the accident with his calm approach—so calm, in fact, that he remembers to ask about the oat test. Of course, there is a double joke on Helga in the final quip, since Carl makes it appear that the oat sample is at least as important as she is. We may now go back to the original ethnic-joke banter about Danes being careful and see how it applies to the careful, controlled image which Carl gives himself in his story. He has been true to his ethnic stereotype and has managed to turn Helga's "typical Dane" jibe against her.

But Helga has the last laugh in this sequence. She picks up on the theme of managing machinery. As someone who had no farming experience until she married Carl, and as a woman who has less strength than a man when it comes to controlling large and heavy machinery, she knows that she cannot rebut Carl's story in a direct fashion. Rather, she turns her own lack of control of machinery to her advantage by stressing another type of control which farmwives have:

Helga: *Oh, I'll tell you now. This is not historic. This is nowadays' farmwives. Green as grass. Of course in no time flat, I was the willing little helper around here. Hadn't driven a truck. Never done anything. And first summer here, I was sitting on the truck and baling. Now I don't know—are you from a farming background?*
Taft: *No.*
Helga: *No. Well we have this marvelous machine and, in bygone days, we used to have a piece of plywood behind this thing where all these square pieces of—bales of hay came out. And hubby was standing one [stack of hay] up, and sliding along [on the plywood] quite happily—*
Carl: *You'd stack them up—*
Helga: *Stack them up.*
Carl: *—eight or ten bales. Give them a bit of a push, and, on this smooth plywood, they'd push off and stand in a stack of eight or ten bales. And then you'd pile some more. Carry on.*
Helga: *So I was driving, but my clutch control wasn't too terribly good. So every time he went sort of—he had to stop.*

And so I let go and it went whump! I mean that tractor leaped. It didn't move—it leaped. And with it leaped the baler, and with it leaped the piece of plywood. And there he had eight bales so carefully stacked, and with it went my hubby and they all ended up in a ditch. And that was it. And finally he stopped it, and he came to the front. And I'm telling you, the language—I'm not going to repeat it. And I says very sweetly, "If you can do it by yourself, I go home." And that was it. He never again complained, because he knew he couldn't do it by himself, and anything was better than nothing. But I tell you, you get a bunch of farmwives together—what they hate about farming. I remember one day hubby came home. . . . He's soaking wet. He goes out seeding. He finds the wettest pothole there is, with a truck full of grain. Comes home and he says, "Dear, do you think you can pull me out?" And that is horrible.

Elsie: *That's about the worst thing.*

Helga: *Isn't it? They come and they put you on this tractor . . . . [much laughter] So you got a logging chain that had links about yea big. Seated up there. And he says, "When I go like this [make a signal] you slowly, slowly pull me out." So you sit in there and you turn around and you're nervous as heck, you know. Waiting for this [signal]. And he goes like this, and your foot goes whump! That's right. It scoots forward and the logging chain goes ping! And your husband goes purple.*

Helga's two stories are a complex rebuttal to her husband's tale. On one level, her tactic is to portray Carl as a man who loses control and whose careful habits are all for naught. Thus, after being thrown into the ditch, it is *Carl's* language which is frantic and uncontrolled. Helga, on the contrary, speaks softly, sweetly, and above all calmly: "I says very sweetly . . ." Similarly, after Helga has snapped the logging chain, her husband loses his composure and "goes purple." Thus, we see Carl in a less than heroic light in these tales. As to his Danish penchant for being careful, Helga again turns the tables on her husband. She makes of point of describing her husband's handiwork: the bales "so carefully stacked." The image is one of a man who is perhaps too meticulous at his task. When he and the bales are thrown into the ditch, the effect is all the more comical in light of this meticulousness. One is reminded of the slapstick comedies of the silent movie era. Similarly, Helga describes her husband's misfortune in getting his grain truck stuck as though he carefully planned his predicament: "He finds the wettest pothole there is"—as if Carl considered with great care and deliberation exactly which pothole was best to get stuck in. Thus, whereas Carl's image of the careful Dane is of one who is calm and in control, Helga's portrayal is of an overmeticulous man who cares only about being careful.

It is interesting to note Carl's interruption in Helga's first story, for it is a part of the general banter between them. Note that he interrupts to explain exactly how the baling operation works. He shows mastery of the machinery through his clear description, while Helga's somewhat confused attempt to describe the process and her flippant and sarcastic attitude towards the machinery ("this marvelous machine") indicates a less comfortable approach to farm machinery. Once Carl has made his point, he relinquishes the floor to his wife with a simple, overly-courteous "Carry on." Here he shows verbal mastery in that he seems to be in control of the conversation even though it is his wife who is the storyteller at that moment.

But Helga's main rebuttal also involves verbal control. After describing Carl's unrepeatable (uncontrolled) language, she gains the upper hand by offering to let him do the baling himself. The quip hits home since both she and her husband know that the wife is an equal partner in agricultural work and that the farm or ranch cannot be run without her help. Her simple statement says volumes about the necessary relationship between husband and wife on a family-run farm. Thus, who is in real control on the farm? The answer, as is evident in Helga's story, is that both husband and wife have equal control, since neither can run the farm without the other.

Of course, this small battle of the sexes was all in fun and was taken as part of the evening's entertainment. Indeed, I doubt that Helga and Carl were conscious of the complexity of their verbal dueling. Many of the points that they scored against each other were done so in an intuitive fashion. From years of working together on the ranch, they know instinctively that a constant battle goes on, by both men and women, against machines; they know the dangers of being overconfident or smug (that is, "careful") in an occupation which is prone to sudden reversals in fortune; and they are well aware of the roles which both husband and wife must play if the ranch is to be successful. This unconscious and unarticulated knowledge lies behind these tales and gives them significance beyond the idle banter which was intended.

The final story of the night grew out of Helga's tale, as the discussion turned to the general problem of mud and stuck vehicles. Carl's telling of this tale is especially humorous because he makes use of yet another stylistic device in his oral delivery: a formula. The theme of the tale is a comedy of errors in which one vehicle after another becomes stuck in an alkali flat. Carl enhances the humour of this incident by repeating, as a sort of punch-line to every segment of his tale, "and he got stuck" (or some variation on this phrase). The formula becomes a refrain for the tale, and every time Carl repeats the phrase, the others chuckle. On occasion, Wes will chime in on this formula refrain, as if Carl were singing a song rather than telling a tale. Such a device does not work well in print, but as delivered orally by Carl, it was a most effective method of bringing out the humour of the situation:

Carl: *Do you remember the time up on the alkali when we had every damn vehicle in the whole countryside stuck?*
Elsie: *Every time someone else came—*
Carl: *I forget who started it off—*
Wes: *John Neufeldt full of grain.*
Carl: *And he went in on the alkali there.*
Wes: *Yeah. Just west of our gate.*
Carl: *And got stuck.*
Wes: *Yeah.*
Carl: *And then—*
Wes: *And then John Wake and old Joshua went down—*
Carl: *With a tractor.*
Wes: *Yeah.*
Carl: *And he got stuck.*

Wes: *He got stuck.*

Carl: *And John went down to pull him out.*

Wes: *Corrie—no, Corrie went down.*

Carl: *Corrie, and then John.*

Wes: *And then John went down, and John wouldn't go near it, because he knew it was alkali. He said he'd have to get a cable.*

Carl: *Yeah. But he got a cable and he got stuck anyway.*

Wes: *And he came down and got a cable at our place. And a cable from another place. And then he got stuck.*

Carl: *And then I heard about all this goings-on, so I took off with the truck to see what was going on, and I got the truck stuck. And I came home and got the tractor and went out there with the tractor, and I got the tractor stuck. Lars come over with his tractor—*

Wes: *Yeah. I didn't know . . .*

Carl: *Didn't he? And got stuck. And Jake brought the D.C. Case over and it got stuck. Everybody—*

Wes: *Yeah.*

Carl: *—was stuck. There was twenty-some odd vehicles—*

Wes: *They were all stuck.*

Carl: *They were all stuck. And Jake finally went home and got an old steel-wheeled tractor. And we'd gone way up into Halcyonia and got Lloyd Northridge's cable and the big rope from his elevator?*

Wes: *Oh yeah.*

Carl: *And then finally we started getting some vehicles out. But anyway it was a community gathering for a few days.*

Carl had taken a simple story of vehicles getting stuck in the mud and, with the help of Wes, turned it into an entertaining comic sketch. His tale was exactly the kind that the evening called for: a true but humorous story about an unusual event or animal or person. Indeed almost all of the stories told that evening shared these two themes: something humorous and something unusual. Of the stories transcribed here, only two were not humorous: the children lost in the blizzard and the filthy living conditions of the squatters. But even the squatter tale was told in a bit of a humorous vein since the Forty-One Seveners have long since departed and their poverty can now be seen as a light-hearted comment on the human condition. As far as the "unusual" is concerned, there are few stories told under any circumstance that concern the usual and everyday events of life. Brushing one's teeth, eating meals, going to work, buying items in a store and the like are not the stuff of tales; only when the routine is broken, only when one is caught in an absurd situation or when one acts in an illogical or unexpected way does a story arise.

The drift of conversation is also worth noting. When we sat down for an evening of talk, we didn't have a schedule of events or an itinerary which we followed. Yet the unspoken rules did keep us on track; or at least the conversation never changed so radically that one could easily isolate one section of the conversation from the next. Rather, the talk shifted and drifted comfortably from local character sketches to personal experience stories to bits of history to tales of extraordinary events to accounts of the lives of those in the room. A word or image in one tale would spark the next as the entire group engaged in free association from tale to tale. For example, Wes's account of his life led Carl to ask him about a specific episode from the past—the many Joe Walners. One story about wild game, the deer, naturally led to another, the geese. One story about whiskey sparked another. Such is the nature of informal, conversational story-telling. Despite the seeming random nature of the talk, there were rules, themes, and associations which linked one part of the conversation with the next.

But we must return to the fact that this evening's entertainment was not quite "natural". I was observing with a tape recorder, and I was there with the expressed purpose of collecting tales. This strange circumstance probably added considerable structure and uniformity to the evening's entertainment since those present were quite conscious throughout the evening that I was there for stories. Thus, if I had not been present, more digressions and more diverse activities might have taken place. Perhaps the four members of the group would have broken into two separate conversational groups—Helga talking to Elsie and Carl to Wes. Perhaps the general conversation would not have centred so consciously on storytelling; Carl might have exchanged weather information with Wes, or Elsie might have given Helga a recipe. Perhaps there would have been much more movement during the evening with two of the four going into another part of the house. Perhaps the children would have played a more significant role during the evening visit if we weren't so obviously intent on "adult" activity. Whenever one collects folklore, there is the frustration of not knowing how much one affects what one is trying to collect. If there is one consolation, it is that I have been involved in such groups and have spent such evenings of uninterrupted storytelling when simply acting as a "folk", that is, when I was not consciously collecting folklore but merely visiting friends and relatives. Thus, I know that such storytelling sessions do occur when the tape recorder is not present.

But as an observer of the scene in the Christensen household that evening, I learned much about their way of living. Some of their speech was rather esoteric and curious to one who did not share their background: "buckbrush," "bluff," "posted" land, "field shelter-belts," "Forty-One Sevener," "dug-out," "bulk station," "heavy clay," "logging chain." Their language has been shaped by their rural and agricultural backgrounds and is as specialized in its own way as is that of the potash miner or the university professor. Their stories also reveal the social expectations of the community. The attitudes towards the old bachelor and the remittance man, the tolerance towards the local moonshiners, the neighborly help afforded during blizzards or when one is stuck in the mud, the value placed on cooking, baking and other home crafts, and the equality of husband and wife on family-run farms were revealed in the stories told that evening. One could hardly expect more if one attended a sociology lecture on Saskatchewan life.

After Carl's story of the alkali affair, the tape recorder clicked, indicating that another side of tape was full. The click seemed to signal an end to the two and a half hours of storytelling (again the intrusion of the observer!), and I took my leave of the Christensens and Ingrams shortly after. But I took with me a valuable document and a gift from these people—their stories. One might say that there was nothing special in this storytelling session since one could visit any home and collect an equally full evening's worth of local tales. But this view misses the point. Such evenings are valuable *because* they occur so often; their value lies in their necessary and integral function within communities and groups. Such story sessions are an essential part of socializing, of forming friendships and bonds within communities, and they are the vehicle for traditions and memories which keep a community united.

4

The St. Laurent Pilgrimage:
A Religious Ritual of Faith and Healing

If you were to travel a few kilometres upstream from Batoche on July 15th or 16th, you would notice some remarkable activities along the western bank. People would be involved in prayer, processions, vigils and masses; you would notice priests hearing confessions, blessing religious objects, and preaching sermons. You might hear religious music or announcements of various sorts from loudspeakers strung from poles and trees in the area. You would see religious statues and symbols, buildings of various kinds, a pavillion and man-made grotto set among the natural scene of the river bank. Above all, you would notice people, hundreds of people attending to these activities or sitting by pitched tents and campers or gathering in groups to talk and visit. If you could enter their conversations, you would as likely hear Cree, French, Polish, or German as you would English. You might also notice that perhaps half of the people were Indian or Metis. You would be witnessing a ritual.

A ritual is a form of communal expression. A group of like-minded people gather in a certain place at a certain time to perform a series of activities. These activities, which make up the customs observed at a ritual, are usually rather structured, often symbolic of some commonly-held attitude or belief, expressing the significance or reason for the gathering. Those who attend the ritual generally know their part in this group performance and have a clear sense of the "agenda" which is to be followed for the ritual to be a success. But beyond understanding the mechanics of performing this group activity, each individual is aware of what the ritual symbolizes, of why the people have taken time off from their daily pursuits to act out some time-honoured, oft-repeated celebration.

The pilgrimage to the shrine of Our Lady of Lourdes at St. Laurent is an example of one such ritual native to Saskatchewan. Indeed, it is probably the oldest gathering of its kind in the province and is related so closely to the historical roots of Saskatchewan that, beyond its religious significance, it might be seen as an annual re-enactment of the province's past. But of course its main importance is that it is an annual gathering of Roman Catholics from around Saskatchewan to reaffirm their faith and perhaps to partake of the healing powers associated with the shrine. This ritual, then, not only represents a part of Saskatchewan's historical and religious heritage but is one facet of traditional medicine in the province.

But what has made this bit of land called St. Laurent a place for gathering, a place for ritual? The answer to this question is not simple; it involves historical, religious, cultural, and even "magical" or "miraculous" factors. Historically, St. Laurent is at the very centre of early Saskatchewan trade and settlement. Located on the western bank of the South Saskatchewan River a few kilometres north of Duck Lake and Batoche, and east of Fort Carlton, it was a stopping place for traders, missionaries and native people in the early nineteenth century. Indeed, mass was first celebrated on the St. Laurent site as early as 1842 when Father Jean-Baptiste Thibault stopped there on his way to Fort Carlton.[1]

In 1870 a group of Metis migrated from Manitoba and established a settlement called Petite Ville near St. Laurent; three years later, this settlement moved to the present site. Thereafter, St. Laurent became the spiritual focal point for the Metis, Indians, and other Roman Catholics in that part of Saskatchewan, as the present director of the shrine, Father Gilles Doucette, explains: "And the St. Laurent Mission, as it was then referred to, became the mother church of all the other settlements around, such as Duck Lake, Batoche itself—Prince Albert even."[2] Inevitably, St. Laurent became involved in both the Northwest Rebellion and the rift between the followers of Louis Riel and the established church. The missionaries of St. Laurent were taken from there and held at Batoche during the uprising, but the settlement itself seemed immune from the fighting that was going on around it:

Father Doucette: *It almost seemed as if—you know, some of the priests will claim that Our Lady protected Her little corner from . . . being affected by the rebellion.*

Of course the settlement was not entirely unaffected by the events of the 1880s. The ill feeling between the church and the native people was partly responsible for the decline of the settlement during the nineteenth and early twentieth centuries. Father Doucette points out, however, that in the late 1880s there were differences between the native people and Father Fourmond, head of the mission, over his methods of religious instruction; consequently, the native people established a school across the river from St. Laurent, which greatly reduced the importance of the mission to the native community. The men of the surrounding communities tended to stay away from the St. Laurent church for these reasons, and, in Father Doucette's words, the mission became a "women's church." However, in the late 1930s, the old tensions eased enough for the men to return to the St. Laurent church, and the mission began its revival as a spiritual centre for the native community.

However, despite the ups and downs of St. Laurent as a settlement, the shrine remained a constant place of ritual. While the historical and cultural importance of the church of St. Laurent waxed and waned over the years, faith in the sacredness of the place did not change. Thus, we must look beyond the history of the settlement in order to understand the vitality of this pilgrimage. The shrine itself came about almost by accident rather than through the urging or planning of the established church hierarchy. Indeed the founder of the shrine (as opposed to the founder of the settlement) was not a priest but a lay brother of the church:

Father Doucette: *Then in early 1879, the Oblate priests being in charge of the settlement also had what they called "brothers" in their orders. And one of those brothers, Brother Piquet, came down from France. And his home town was Lourdes, where there had been the figure, the apparition of the Blessed Virgin. And he had known Bernadette, who was the little girl who had seen the Blessed Virgin in Lourdes. They had gone to school together and they had gone to catechism together, so he knew her as very close in childhood. And when Brother Piquet arrived here at St. Laurent settlement, the whole area really spoke to him of his home town of Lourdes. And the idea came to him also to sort of maybe create a little Lourdes right here in Canada. Because by that time, the apparition of the Blessed Virgin had become quite world-wide known, you know. And a lot were flocking to Lourdes in France, and there was quite a big shrine built up. And the whole scenery of St. Laurent reminded him of his home town.*

Not only the scenery reminded Brother Piquet of Lourdes. The natural spring of water on the site also seemed reminiscent of that place of ritual in his native France. As we shall see, this spring came to play an important part in the ritual. But Brother Piquet did not necessarily envision the pilgrimage which was to grow from his inspiration; other factors combined to turn Piquet's idea into a large and important ritual, as Father Doucette goes on to explain:

And a day or so after he arrived here, he started a little prayer corner of his own, where he cleared a few little trees— underbrush—and cleared up one of the trees so he could place a picture of Our Lady of Lourdes in the tree. And then in 1881 . . . Miss Dorval, which was one of the first school teachers in Saskatchewan, a certified teacher in Saskatchewan, arrived here in St. Laurent to help—then Father Fourmond was in charge of the settlement—in starting up his school. And one of the first things that Father Fourmond spoke to Miss Dorval [about] was to lead her to this little place that Brother Piquet had started as a prayer corner, and invited her to come and to pray with the children on this prayer corner. And he must have also made a remark that the picture that Brother Piquet had placed in [the tree] had been quite weather-beaten, and so forth. So Father Fourmond gave her a little statue of Our Lady of Pontmain . . . . . And then from that time on, Brother Piquet and the children of the mission—even the people of the mission— would come down and say a certain amount of prayer around the prayer corner.

Thus, a combination of the established church, represented by Father Fourmond, and the laity—Brother Piquet, Miss Dorval, and the mission children—turned a small inspirational and private place of prayer into a public "prayer corner" in the settlement. Given the rift between the church and the community at that time, the secular, non-establishment nature of the prayer corner (as opposed to the mission church itself) undoubtedly contributed to the development of the ritual. But these factors still do not entirely explain why St. Laurent became a place of ritual.

Before St. Laurent could be seen by the community as a site for pilgrimage, as a place to reaffirm one's faith in God and to receive His help, there had to be some sign that the place was in some way "special." Certainly this is the case with all of the world's great shrines, including Lourdes in France; some miracle or some act of great religious significance must be attached to a site before it can become a place of ceremony and healing. Although St. Laurent is not world-renowned as a place where an event of dramatic religious significance took place, it shares with the great shrines of the world a sense of magic, mystery, or the miraculous. The healing properties of the prayer corner at St. Laurent first became apparent in 1884, as Father Doucette explains:

And Brother Piquet became quite friendly with Mr. Charles Nolin, who was then the Member of Parliament for the west. And his wife had been ill for quite a few years—and they had a family of nine or ten children—and she was going blind, and also [she had] loss of blood, hemorrhaging. And she had seen quite a few doctors, and they had given her up as hopeless. And Brother Piquet sort of mentioned to Charles Nolin that they should start a novena to Our Lady of Lourdes. And he had water from Lourdes. And with the idea that if they obtained the cure for his wife, that he [Nolin] would purchase the first statue he needed for his little prayer corner—one of the bigger statues. So in late December, they started the novena to Our Lady of Lourdes, and on the ninth day, Mrs. Nolin was completely cured. Now you can go back to the history books to verify this. And then Mr. Nolin kept his promise. And the first big statue that you see on your way down to the grotto is the one that was purchased by Mr.

The Grotto

Charles Nolin's Statue

Nolin, and was really the first statue of the grotto. The first grotto built around the statue of Mrs. Nolin and Mr. Nolin dates back to about 1909.

The spontaneous cure of Mrs. Nolin's illness was the sign to others that St. Laurent was indeed a special place. What added even further significance to this miraculous healing was that Mr. and Mrs. Nolin were important, respectable members of the community—the very people who could convince sceptical clergy and laymen alike of the Lourdes-like qualities of Brother Piquet's prayer corner. As well, the statue of the Virgin Mary which Nolin donated to the site was a material statement of belief around which others could affirm their faith in God and, more specifically, in the healing powers of God.

The healing may well have been enough to ensure that St. Laurent would become a shrine, but a further incident reinforced the belief of the community in the sacred nature of the site:

L'année 1890, pendant l'octave de la Fête-Dieu, il se passa un fait extraordinaire dans la mansarde de l'ancien couvent. Sur la cloison à droite de l'escalier, on vit se dessiner l'ombre d'une grande croix portant nettement tracés les contours du Divin Crucifié. Elle semblait projetée la par le rayon du soleil qui s'engouffrait par la fenêtre ouverte. Mlle Odile Pelletier, qui était témoin de ce phénomène avec ses petits pensionnaires, chercha autour d'elle une explication plausible. N'en trouvant pas, elle envoya avertir le P. Fourmond. Ce bon Père, tout ému de ce qu'il voyait, les fit tous mettre à genoux, disant: "C'est mystérieux. Prions;" et il pria quelque temps avec eux. Le même fait se renouvela pendant plusiers jours consécutifs.

[In 1890, during the octave of the feast of Corpus Christi, an extraordinary event took place in the attic of the old convent. On the wall to the right of the stairway there appeared a shadow of a large cross and the outline of the crucified Christ. The shadow seemed to be cast by the rays of the sun that streamed from an open window. Miss Odile Pelletier, who along with her students witnessed this

phenomenon, tried to find some plausible explanation for this shadow, but she could find none. She sent word of this phenomenon to Father Fourmond. The Father, greatly moved by what he saw, made them all kneel down, and said, "It is a mystery. Let us pray." And for some time he prayed with them. The same phenomenon recurred for several days in succession.][3]

Different people have attached different meanings to this apparition. Father Fourmond himself saw it as an omen of the decline of the settlement. Father Doucette sees it as a legend of St. Laurent which some take seriously while others do not—"[The people today] look at it more and more as a story"—and he does not consider the apparition to be an important factor in the development of the shrine. However, this story is widely known among the pilgrims and has become a part of the fabric of mystery and sacredness of the site. Even those who are somewhat hazy as to the details of the phenomenon readily associate the apparition with the history and significance of St. Laurent. Here is the account of one long-time pilgrim, Joseph Greyeyes:

There was an apparition here, I think, years ago. And more or less there was a school here someplace. I couldn't recall where it was. Anyway there was a school and there was, I think, quite a few Indians in there. There was quite a few Indians and their kids were going to school in Duck Lake and they used to bring them to church here. My dad was in there and my mother was there. Yeah, they were all here.
Taft: *What kind of apparition?*
Greyeyes: *The apparition, I guess, they seen something in the clouds. Something like that, you see. They figured it was the Blessed Virgin or something.*[4]

Perhaps, for the pilgrims the facts of the event are not as important as is the significance of the event: a sign that St. Laurent was a sacred place, a place of ritual. Such a sign could only reinforce or heighten the perception of the site as a "special place."

Thus, many factors combined to make St. Laurent a place of ritual: the historical significance of the site (especially to the native people), the lay or secular origins of the shrine, the miraculous healing of a well-known personage, and the stories of the apparition. Perhaps the ritual could not have developed from any one of these factors alone but grew out of this combination of events. Indeed many shrines and sacred places result from a combination of history, mystery, and the charisma of one person.

But what is the nature of this ritual? What does the average pilgrim do when he reaches St. Laurent? The activities or customs of this religious ritual are many, but they generally fall into two groups: those "official activities" organized by the church and marked on the calendar or schedule for pilgrims to follow, and those unofficial activities which, though not rigidly scheduled or conducted by the clergy, make up an important part of the ritual. Father Doucette outlines the official activities of the pilgrimage:

You know, it's quite a traditional thing, you know. We start off on Wednesday evening, the 15th in the evening, for what we call the penitential celebration, which is the regular confession which every pilgrim will try to go to while they are at the shrine. They usually start off with this—you know, a time of repentance where they ask forgiveness for their failures. And in the past few years we've had the Marian Hours—it's always been, but maybe not in as organized a form as we have now—where people really join in and sing the rosary. You know, rosary after rosary is said. Followed by the mass—the eucharistic celebration—and then there's the torchlight procession which really intrigues a lot of people and brings a lot of people, which is a ceremony in the dark with candlelight. Very impressive, and I think that it's a moment when they really feel close to God. And then for the last three years, we've had all-night adoration vigils, where there's a continuous recitation of the rosary in front of the Blessed Sacrament. And we rely a lot on the campers that they come up during the night and spend an hour or so, so that there's always some people [there], and the recitation of the rosary is continuous throughout the whole night. And then the next day we keep on with the celebration of the mass. We have a mass in Cree, a mass in French, a mass in English and a celebration in Polish. . . . And then the traditional thing is the Stations of the Cross, which is quite a highlight, and then the eucharistic procession of the Blessed Sacrament, ending with the blessing of the sick and the blessing of the water which people bring back home from the source.

Beyond the orderliness and planning which characterize these official activities, such customs allow for the entire religious community to act "as one." Such highly structured parts of the ritual necessarily give the pilgrims a sense of solidarity, a feeling that they share beliefs with those from other communities, cultures, generations, or classes. The processions, masses, and adorations are a form of communal drama in which each pilgrim plays a role and, more importantly, in which one is aware of one's relationship to the entire religious community. The great crowd at the pilgrimage is an impressive sight, and many pilgrims include this sight among their earliest memories of St. Laurent. In such a throng, one loses one's sense of individuality, but counterbalancing that loss is the gain of being accepted and playing an important part in the gathering of pilgrims. For example, a pilgrim who takes part in the all-night vigil becomes aware that each individual's solitary effort has been necessary in order to create the communal rite of adoration; each pilgrim is a link in the chain of prayer which lasts throughout the night.

But the official activities also allow for personal honour and achievement. Although each pilgrim plays a role in the celebration, some roles have greater status than others. Obviously, the priests have the status of religious leaders within the ritual, but there are also roles performed by the laity which might be termed "high profile." Carrying a cross or banner in a procession is one such role, and the high status of this responsibility is clearly reflected in Joseph Greyeyes' story:

I can tell you this much: my uncle was an elderly man. He was on each pilgrimage from the time—you might say his father started the pilgrimage here. He was along all the time too. And to tell you the truth, he carried the cross for forty years in this pilgrimage here. So that's quite a commendation for us, I guess.

The Procession of the Blessed Sacrament

Pilgrims coming to confession

Joseph Greyeyes' story, however, indicates another point of individual pride among pilgrims: the number of pilgrimages and the number of consecutive pilgrimages attended. Many pilgrims boast of coming to St. Laurent for thirty, forty, or even fifty years, and many can name the exact years when they *didn't* attend, whether because of work, war, or illness.

However, no individual is entirely subsumed by the group at this pilgrimage. The unofficial activities of the ritual speak to the individual pilgrim's achievements, failures, and personal faith in a way which would be impossible for the official, structured parts of the celebration to do. Personal prayer, of course, is one example of an unofficial tradition which is as old as or even older than the official activities at the shrine and is, by definition, a solitary rather than communal custom. Thus, throughout the two days of the celebration, one can see pilgrims kneeling, praying, or lighting candles in front of the Nolin statue, at the grotto, at the Stations of the Cross, or at other places on the site. The Nolin statue of the Virgin Mary is especially popular in this respect, and many pilgrims will not pass by the site without at least some sign of personal devotion towards the statue.

But there are more dramatic personal acts of faith associated with the ritual. Among the oldest and most popular unofficial customs is the walk from Duck Lake to the shrine, as Father Doucette explains:

Most of the native people—you'll see very few white people—mostly the native people are the ones that walk. Like see, they come from Beardy [Reserve]. They'll drive to Duck Lake and from Duck Lake they'll fan out and walk all the way, the seven or eight miles to the shrine. And that is still quite active among the native people. Very few white people do it, though. But there's also a reservation across the river here, the One Arrow, and quite a few of them walk down too. It's mostly popular among the native people. And also from other reservations. And you see, the idea really came from the school, the Indian school in Duck Lake. Most of the natives from Mistawasis, from Muskeg, the Leask area, and the One Arrow actually went to school at St. Michael's in Duck Lake,

*and that's where they became aware of this. And that's where
the idea of walking to the shrine became part of the custom,
the tradition.*

Michel Fortier attributes the origin of the walk to an earlier
period in St. Laurent's history, but the two versions are not
necessarily contradictory; the earlier event might have
inspired the teachers at St. Michael's School to take the walk:

*A lay-brother, Brother Guillet, of Reindeer Lake, who was
crippled from a wound in his leg, made a novena and a
pilgrimage to the shrine. There on September 21, 1893, his
leg was cured and he was able to return to hard work at the
Reindeer Lake Mission. As a result of this event the custom of
walking from Duck Lake to St. Laurent began.*[5]

This personal act, considered by most pilgrims to be a
traditional sign of faith or perhaps a way or reliving a part of
the shrine's history, may sometimes be extended into an act
of penance. Pilgrims Sara and Fred Bouchard give one
example:

Sara: *And my dad one time, he walked from Leask all the
way to the shrine. He wore out two pair of moccasins;
halfways, he changed them.*
Taft: *Well, why did he walk? Was there some kind of reason?*
Fred: *Well, it was penance, like.*
Sara: *My brothers, three of them passed away—there was
three of them within a month. So he had to make that
promise [to do penance]. So he walked from Leask right up
till Duck Lake here that same day. He camped there. There
were holes in his moccasins, so he changed them and he
walked up here.*
Taft: *Must have been a long walk.*
Sara: *Yeah.*
Fred: *Tell him what he had to eat.*
Sara: *He just had lemons all the way. . . .*
Fred: *Fasting like, you know.*[6]

Walking to the shrine, then, may be done for traditional
reasons or for some specific purpose, but in either case it

represents an individualistic act rather than a communal one. The walk allows the pilgrims to express their own problems and troubles within the context of the ritual as a whole:

Father Doucette: *I think a lot of native people, they want a special favour. Also [they] have a great devotion. And they sort of promise throughout the year that they'll walk to the shrine. You know, if they ask a certain favour of Mary, they'll make a promise throughout the whole of the year that next year they'll walk to the shrine. . . . That's how come it's kept up too; because a lot of the young people do it as a student. I think it becomes part of their culture, part of their belief also.*

In a sense, then, the penance walk or the walk to express thankfulness is similar to the personal prayers at the shrine: an unofficial activity which answers individual needs and beliefs.

The unofficial activities, however, are not limited to acts of faith. Indeed all of the activities discussed so far refer to the sacred side of the ritual. But there are many activities associated with the shrine that are quite secular in deed and function. These unofficial activities centre on the ritual as an annual gathering of people rather than the ritual as an annual show of faith. These unofficial customs include the trip to St. Laurent, camping and eating, and visiting friends.

Pilgrims readily recall their early experiences in travelling to the shrine. Before the days of paved roads and fast cars or trucks, the trip was both an adventure and an ordeal. For many families, the trip was a two-day affair, and the means of transportation was a wagon and a team of horses:

Joseph Greyeyes: *The first few years we come over here in the 20s, right down to the 40s, we used to come down here just with a team of horses and camp on our way down. It's quite a distance, you know, for horses to come over here. And sometimes we had our own work to do for about half a day, and then we'd start in the afternoon, you see, and proceed for the shrine. . . . .Well it would take us about, let's see, pretty well the full day. Yeah, pretty well the full day.*

Taft: *So you didn't have to camp over night on the way there?*

Greyeyes: *Yes, yes, we did sometimes. Sometimes when we used to leave home in the afternoons, well we couldn't make it in one day. Because you see it all depends; the weather too, you see. Sometimes we had to stop due to the rain, you see. And other times, being so warm, so hot, it's very difficult to use the horses. We didn't want to abuse the horses, [in] the first place, to bring them along that distance. So then we finally got here and then we put up our tents. And then after we get through putting up our tents, well then we all go down to the shrine.*

Sara Bouchard: *My family, we all used to bring them with a wagon, you know, a big wagon like this. . . .*

Fred: *You seen these pioneers sometimes with covered wagons?*

Sara: *The kids, you know, they used to stay under there when it rains. They weren't wet. When it's hot, they were warm. . . .*

Taft: *How long did it take you to get down here?*

Sara and Fred: *A day and a half.*

There were certain spots along the river which were traditional half-way camps for the pilgrims, becoming in a sense small, secular sites attached to the ritual at St. Laurent:

Joseph Greyeyes: *You have to stop off on the way down, you know. . . . We used to come across Carlton's Ferry most of the time and then we used to either stop across the ferry or else just about the other side of the ferry approximately a mile or a mile and a half or so. Yeah, some nice flats there. Well you see, there's also a lot of open space where your horse will eat, you see. And you hobble your horses. . . . Sometimes there was half a dozen tents or something like that . . . just in one place.*

Of course, in recent years this unofficial activity has been reduced to a short, uneventful car trip, but the two-day trip to St. Laurent remains a part of the collective memory of the pilgrims. However, although the trip is now short, the tents,

A Pilgrim's campsite

store-bought rather than handmade, and motorized campers increasingly ubiquitous, the general secular act of camping out has remained a constant at the ritual. Indeed if one could do the impossible—that is, ignore the pervasive religious atmosphere and activity of the site—St. Laurent might appear to be nothing more than another summer campground for tourists: families sitting around campers and tents; barbecues, picnic baskets, and coolers filled with drinks; brightly-coloured lawn furniture; casual summer clothes complete with sunhats, shorts, T-shirts, and sunglasses; children playing on the grass or in the sand; people strolling through the woods.

But the religious side of the ritual cannot be ignored, and all of these secular, unofficial activities are incidental to the reasons for the gathering. Indeed, although one of the functions of the pilgrimage is to socialize and visit with friends and relatives, few pilgrims would give this function first priority. Joseph Greyeyes, for example, understands that socializing certainly plays a part in the ritual, but he places this function second to that of religious duty and, more importantly, sees the socializing as a reaffirmation of the religious faith of the community:

The reason why we used to bring our family here is more or less to continue with the religion. You know, to continue with their religion. We were trying to show them [the children] the right path, you see. If they don't see us, if we leave this world, some of them might follow—there's always some trace of something else, you see. Anyway, they [his children] been pretty regular too, but they live so far away now, see. They're all over different places. . . . The reason why we used to come here too is more or less there's lots of people we haven't seen for years. . . . And they're our relatives and one thing and another. First is church, and then you do the visiting, you see [laughs]. . . . Oh yes, yes, we were very interested to see people that [we] haven't seen for a couple of years or so, and maybe five years or more, you see. It all depends. Some of them used to come way down from Meadow Lake and Green Lake and all these areas. And then they were just as happy as we were, you know, to see them here. It's an ideal place for them to see you, you see. See that they still continue with their religion.

Sara and Fred Bouchard gave socializing absolutely no priority and were quite single-minded in their approach to the ritual:

Taft: *Are there other reasons for coming here besides the religious? Do you meet people here?*
Fred: *Well—*
Sara: *No, not exactly. We come here to honour our Mother [the Virgin Mary]. That's how I feel. I don't—well if I see somebody . . . but we're here to come and pray.*

Indeed, although St. Laurent is of necessity a campground, it does not invite secular socializing. Father Doucette recalls another shrine where there was a lake and where the surroundings were pleasant enough that one might easily forget the reasons for the pilgrimage. But at St. Laurent, the river is not accessible for swimming, and the upper level of the bank where the campground is located is hot and dusty and, in a word, functional. The most beautiful and inviting part of St. Laurent is not the campground but the lower bank at the grotto and at the Stations of the Cross.

99

Thus, the very setting directs the pilgrim away from secular thoughts and towards devotion.

However, Father Doucette does not reject the socializing function of the pilgrimage; rather, he sees the socializing as an important part of the religious activity of the ritual:

I really feel that people come to pray, you know. There's definitely an exchange of social aspects, but there again I think that's just being human. And I think it's part of praying, you know. Being open to your brother. That's when you start living it out.

Thus, although the pilgrimage is both a sacred and a secular ritual, all activities ultimately have religious significance for the participants.

It is worth noting at this point that just as the sacred and secular parts of the ritual are interconnected, so are the official and unofficial activities of the ritual. As with all folklore, the ritual is not a static, unchanging activity; rather, from year to year, the forces of change work on the celebration so that no one year's ritual is exactly like the next. One indication of the variability of the ritual is that unofficial activities can become official. In outlining the official parts of the celebration, Father Doucette alluded to this phenomenon at least twice: referring to the Marian Hours, he said, "It's always been, but maybe not in as organized a form as we have now"; he also mentioned that the all-night vigil is a recent addition to the official schedule. These two activities, like the walk from Duck Lake, may have deep roots in the history of unofficial customs at the shrine. Certainly, all-night vigils might well have been practised by individual pilgrims for penance or thankfulness. That they are now official parts of the ritual does not necessarily diminish their significance to individual pilgrims, but it does establish their importance as a part of the communal celebration.

Beyond the primary function of the ritual as a reaffirmation of faith (and its very secondary function of socializing), why is this pilgrimage such an important ritual for those who participate in it? Does this ritual have other functions? Certainly it functions to promote "togetherness" in at least two ways: it is a place in which native people can re-establish ties and assert their sense of common culture, and it is a place in which family members can express their mutual bonds and obligations to each other.

Although the ritual is meant for all Roman Catholics, there is no doubt in any pilgrim's mind that the shrine is especially meaningful for the native people. As discussed earlier, this part of Saskatchewan, and the settlement of St. Laurent in particular, is of great historical importance to the Indians and Metis. But history, culture, and religion are not so easily separated; thus, St. Laurent is also of cultural and religious significance to the Indians and Metis. Father Doucette's repeated observation that the Duck Lake walk is a ceremony for native people is one indication of the special meaning of this ritual for the Indians and Metis. But in more general and unspecified ways, native pilgrims assert the cultural significance of the ritual:

Father Doucette: *For a lot of natives, that's what their religion is all about is the shrine really. They may not be church-goers in the rest of the year, but they wouldn't miss the shrine for all the money in the world. It's a moment when they really reconcile with God and get close to God. You know, it's a meaningful thing. They're also very close to the Blessed Virgin, you know. They have a very strong devotion to Mary. . . . I think the reason is the Oblate Fathers; the Oblate Fathers is really an order that has Mary as one of their main devotion[s]. . . . They're Oblates of Mary Immaculate. And therefore, naturally, they spread the devotion to Mary quite strongly, and they were the first missionaries that really went out to the natives and therefore brought Mary along with them.*

Here again, history and religion have mixed to create a culturally significant ritual. The historical fact of the Oblate missionary work among the Indians makes a shrine devoted to the Virgin Mary especially important to the native people. Joseph Greyeyes also makes the connection between the shrine and early missionary work among the Indians:

I think the natives started this more than any other nationality. Because the Indians, the first Indians, and the

101

first missionaries, they were working with the Indians so much that they got them interested. They were strong Catholics, you know. Strong Catholics, the natives. And then from there on, you see, they [the missionaries] preached and so forth. Well you see, years ago there used to be good preaching from these missionaries, and you'd feel that, you see. You'd feel that in yourselves: "Well they've given us a good preaching. Why should we turn it down? Let's go for it. Let's tend to all these things." So then I would say that it's the natives who more or less started this pilgrimage, you see.

Perhaps one important factor here is that the white Roman Catholics—the Poles, the Germans, the French, the Irish—can look to the European roots of both their religion and culture, whereas the roots of the native people are here in Saskatchewan. Rome and the Old World religion are especially distant to those who are native to the New World; thus, St. Laurent is closer to home in more ways than one for the Indians and Metis.

Like many other rituals throughout the year, the pilgrimage is a time for the reunification of the family group, for a general sense of family. The family is an important topic of conversation among pilgrims; how many in one's family have come this year; who has not been able to make it; how one is carrying on the family tradition of attending. The ritual as a family affair often becomes evident in the pilgrims' reminiscences:

Joseph Greyeyes: *I was, let's see, just a minute—seventeen years old. Yeah . . . my dad had passed away already, but I was too young. I was in school when they started their pilgrimage here. But in 1922, I started to bring my mother and then I wasn't married till '27. See I used to bring my mother down for the pilgrimage. And then after I got married, I started bringing my wife. Naturally as the years go by, well we raised a family, you see. And then our children, we brought our children along.*

The continuity from parent to child in attending the ritual expresses the continuity of family life itself. With each pilgrimage, the cohesiveness of the family structure is renewed, as each pilgrim thinks back to when they were taken by their parents, to when they took their parents, to when they brought their own family, to when their children brought their grandchildren, to when they were taken by their children—the chain of obligation to both the shrine and to family members continues:

Sara Bouchard: *Now it's my family that's grown, and they all come here and bring their families.*
Taft: *When did you first bring your children here? When they were very young?*
Sara: *Oh when they were babies [laughs].*
Fred: *Yeah, we brought one here when she was two weeks old.*
Sara: *She was baptized here. That's my youngest one.*

The function, however, which is foremost in the minds of many pilgrims and which is perhaps the most dramatic aspect of the entire ritual is the healing function of the shrine. Many come to St. Laurent specifically to be cured of a disease while others find that "feeling better" is a happy by-product of their devotions to the shrine. In either case, the shrine acts as a form of traditional medicine for those who attend, and it can be seen as a part of the folk medical heritage of Saskatchewan.

For those who have received no benefit from medical doctors or who, for whatever reason, place no faith in the "official" medical establishment, the shrine is an alternative for treatment. Such an alternative is not surprising, considering that in many cultures there is little differentiation made between medicine and religion: the "priest" is both a spiritual leader and a medical practitioner. Many medical doctors at least tacitly agree to the connection between their craft and religion when they recognize the importance of the emotional and mental disposition of their patients in effecting a cure. Faith in God as an emotional and mental state can have a considerable bearing on the health of the individual.

But before one can understand the role of healing at the shrine, one must understand the true extent of the ritual. Up to this point, the ritual has been discussed as though it were a two-day affair or at most a week-long celebration, if one includes the trip to and from St. Laurent. In fact, the ritual is a year-long celebration for the pilgrims. Throughout the year, pilgrims recall past pilgrimages and anticipate the coming celebration. In effect, the memories, the anticipation, and the actual preparation for the trip are as important as the participation in the activities of July 15th and 16th. The two-day celebration is merely the culmination of a year-long ritual.

The material manifestations of this year-long celebration are the religious articles which the pilgrims purchase at St. Laurent. This unofficial activity borders on the official, since the church has established a store on the grounds where such items can be bought:

Father Doucette: *People have so little access to religious articles. You know, most of your stores won't carry them. Except maybe your local stores are starting to carry them. But it was something that was quite hard for most people to get, and this was sort of an occasion when they could stock up on all sorts of the religious articles as gifts throughout the year. It's been part of the custom of the shrine to sort of stock up on religious articles.*

Rosaries, medals, crucifixes, holy pictures, pins, statues, candles—these are the material folklore of the pilgrimage, and they play an important part in the year-long nature of the ritual. Many pilgrims buy them as keepsakes or as evidence of having attended the pilgrimage. The articles transport the significance of the shrine from its site at St. Laurent to the home of the pilgrim and in doing so transport the powers of faith from the shrine to the home. For this last reason, it is important that the articles be blessed by a priest— so important that the activity is an official part of the ritual. The practice of Sara and Fred Bouchard illustrates the function of these items as religious keepsakes and as part of the year-long cycle of the ritual:

Taft: *Do you buy souvenirs or things of that sort?*
Sara and Fred: *Oh yeah.*
Taft: *And what do you do with them once they're bought?*

Sara and Fred: *We keep them.*
Sara: *We keep them. I got a little glass cupboard there. All of my souvenirs, they're all placed right in there. Statues, crosses.*
Taft: *Do you give any as gifts? Do you give any to your children?*
Sara: *Sometimes we give them medals and candles.*

Giving the religious articles away as gifts extends the ritual not only through time but through space. For family members who cannot attend, the blessed articles from the shrine become a physical link to the ritual which others have attended. Joseph Greyeyes expands upon this point:

Joseph Greyeyes: *Then we go back and we take home—if we have a little surplus money—we go to work and get some souvenirs from this store here that they sell souvenirs. Well that's been carrying on ever since then. We always get something from down here, from the shrine, and take it home and keep it for a year or so. And then we're here again and we're doing the same thing again. . . . There's all kinds of souvenirs nowadays, more or less. Here's a souvenir I got here.*
Taft: *That's St. Christopher? St. Christopher in the car?*
[We were sitting in the car during the interview].
Joseph: *Yeah sure. I bought it in 1952. Yeah. Well how many years you figure? That's quite a few years. Yes, I've had that in my cars ever since then. And then I always get some new ones. Well my family, my family's spread all over, but I always send them souvenirs from here, you see. I buy a bunch of souvenirs and I send them up there wherever they are. . . . Oh you can get anything. You can get rosaries. Anything. . . . Like you take children: you fancy something that you want to get for your young grandson or young granddaughter and so forth. Well you go to work and pick something out for them. And then before we take them home, they're blessed. We have them blessed, you see. And then we send them down, well, wherever they [his children] are. We always say that they're blessed and so forth.*

Here we see the function of the extended ritual in maintaining family ties, just as does the immediate ritual of July 15th and 16th. As well, Joseph Greyeyes alludes to another function of the religious articles: namely, as good luck pieces or religious charms. The St. Christopher medal in the car guards against accidents. Thus, like healing, religious articles transfer the power of faith to power over the physical world.

The healing function of the shrine relates very closely to the extended nature of the ritual. Sickness occurs throughout the year, but the immediate ritual only lasts two days. Thus, pilgrims need not attend the shrine immediately in order to be cured; they need only promise to attend for the cure to be effective. Note the following account by Joseph Greyeyes:

I feel that I was more or less healed in 1950 due to coming here, you know. Coming to this grotto and one thing and another. You know my stomach—I couldn't work that summer. And then I made a pledge then, regardless what it was, that I'd come to the shrine. And then my stomach went perfect. . . . Well there's little things like that have appeared, you see. And so there's lots of people that come over here for years and years and been feeling not so good, been sick and one thing and another. My God, they're still living. Yeah, yeah, something is holding them up, you see—their religion. They believe in their faith, you see.

The use of the spring water from St. Laurent is related to the use of religious articles, to the extended nature of the ritual, and to the healing function of the shrine. Among the unofficial (or perhaps semi-official) activities at St. Laurent is the obtaining of spring water from a pump at the side of the grotto. Usually there are several children who have the honour of pumping the handle as pilgrims gather around with bottles and jars to collect the water. Many pilgrims bring gallon jugs or used bleach bottles for this purpose.

As they do with the religious articles, the priests bless these bottles of water, and the pilgrims take the bottles home for use throughout the year. Portions of the water might be given to those who did not attend the pilgrimage, to family members and friends, as another keepsake and reminder of the shrine. But the water also has healing properties and thus is part of the healing function of the extended ritual:

Joseph Greyeyes: *I know there's lots been healed, you see. Been healed for coming in here. And you take that blessed water there. You see that water. I always take a little container home and I use it for the whole year. Well sometimes in a pinch you rub that on yourself, like you know [rubs his knee].*
Taft: *If you're feeling sore somewhere?*
Greyeyes: *Yes, when you get sore someplace. Just kind of take some of it and just rub it down there. And my God, next morning you'll feel one hundred percent. Yeah. I know I've been doing that different times and by golly it helped me along. I didn't have to get any medicine or anything, you see. But you know as you get up in years, your body is not as solid as it used to be [laughs].*

However, most documented cases of healing have occurred at the site itself. The healing of Mrs. Nolin and Brother Guillet are only the best known of hundreds of similar cases. Although there has been no effort to record these events in any organized fashion, some have been written down and others have remained in the memories of the priests and pilgrims. The following stories are two of several that are recounted in *Historique du Sanctuaire*:

L'année suivante [1907], affluence toujours croissante; et nouvelles faveurs de Marie. Une femme ruthène de Fish Creek, Madame Jurko Betzkal, agée de 22 ans, fut subitement guérie de tuberculose avancée.

[*The next year [1907], the crowds ever increased [at the shrine]; as did the favours of the Virgin Mary. A Ruthenian woman from Fish Creek, Mrs. Jurko Betzkal, age 22, was suddenly cured of advanced tuberculosis.*] (p. 36)

Le pèlerinage de 1923 fut marqué par la guérison soudaine d'une mère de famille atteinte du mal de Bright. Voici le fait, tel que nous l'a transmis son père: "Nous avons une fille marieé, mère de cinq enfants. Elle suffrait depuis un an et demi d'un mal de rein incurable. Elle était presque continuellement au lit. Cela nous faisait tellement mal au coeur de la voir souffrir que tous ensemble nous avons promis de faire le pélerinage à Notre-Dame de Lourdes de Saint-Laurent. Nous avons tous fait la communion et entendu toutes les messes jusqu'a la dernière. Nous avons fait la procession et, juste au moment où nous avons demandé la guérison des malades et des infirmes, notre fille fut guérie. Alors elle semble perdre toutes ses forces et moi, son père, je fus obligé de la supporter. Nous avons tous versé des larmes de joie et de remerciement à la Vierge de Saint-Laurent. Ma fille est retournée chez elle heureuse et contente; elle ne pouvait pas dormir tant sa joie était grande. Elle ne s'est jamais plus ressentie de ce mal."

[The 1923 pilgrimge was marked by the sudden cure of a wife and mother who was struck by Bright's disease. Here is the account given to us by her father: "We have a married daughter, mother of five children, who suffered for a year and a half from an incurable kidney disease. She was confined to her bed almost all the time. To see her suffer made us so heartsick that we all promised to go on the pilgrimage to Our Lady of Lourdes at St. Laurent. We all took communion and attended the masses from beginning to end. We marched in the procession and, at the very moment when we prayed for the cure of the sick and disabled, our daughter was cured. She seemed to lose all her strength and I, her father, had to support her. We all cried tears of joy and thanksgiving to the Virgin of St. Laurent. My daughter has returned home happy and content; so great was her joy that she couldn't sleep. She has never again felt the effects of her illness."] (pp.42-43)

Cures of this sort not only recurred in the past history of the shrine but continue to occur today. Father Doucette recalls a more recent case:

Just two years ago, as we were going to start the procession, one man came up to me. He was from Alberta. And he wanted to know if he could carry the cross in the procession. And I said, "Yes," and then I asked him why. And he said that the year before he had been there [to the shrine]. The doctor *condemned him that he only had a few months to live—he was dying of cancer—and he had been totally cured through the visit [to the shrine]. And he was coming back in thanksgiving. And I've received other letters of mothers or grandmothers who have prayed for their little children who were allergic to certain things. They were cured totally here at the shrine.*

The healing function of the shrine is its most extraordinary and dramatic feature, but it does not necessarily dominate the other functions of the ritual. Unlike Lourdes in France or Ste. Anne de Beaupré in Quebec, the medical aspect of the pilgrimage does not pervade the entire atmosphere. Although in the past, crutches and canes used to hang from the grotto—a traditional sign of a healing shrine—such sights exist now only in the memories of older pilgrims. There are no great lines of bedridden pilgrims or ambulances bringing the critically ill. During the ceremony of the anointing of the sick, there are no joyous outbursts, no discarding of crutches, nor any sightless eyes that suddenly see. In short, there is not the drama that one might expect of a healing ritual.

Rather, the healing tends to be subtle, personal and, as discussed earlier, not always immediate. For every dramatic case in the literature or in the memories of the pilgrims and priests of a sudden, spectacular cure, there are many cases of small cures of minor, or at least non-critical, illnesses. The case of Sara Bouchard is representative of the more subtle type of healing which occurs at the shrine:

Fred Bouchard: *Well I never seen any [cures] myself. I seen canes in there [the grotto], you know.*
Sara: *Well I used to use canes too.*
Fred: *Yeah.*
Sara: *I remember one time I came. Oh I had a hard time. So I used a cane going down [to the grotto].*
Fred: *She broke both her legs. . . .*
Sara: *But coming up now, I didn't use my canes. I made it. But going down, I had trouble. So I put these old canes down there and I got blessed, I guess. So I made it. And then every year after that, they take me over there with a vehicle, but last*

Anointing the sick

night I made it and I made it back here [to the campsite].
Fred: *A transport backed into her and broke her two legs.*

The easing of pain from an old accident, and the simple
act of being able to walk up the steep incline from the grotto
to the campsite are small triumphs of faith which are
perhaps as important as the dramatic cures. The main
function of the shrine remains the reaffirmation of the
pilgrims' faith, and the healings, both dramatic and subtle,
encourage this reaffirmation. The great cures and the small
cures parallel the official and unofficial activities in their
separate functions. Like the official activities, the great cures
become stories which all pilgrims share—the cure of Mrs.
Nolin, for example—and which all pilgrims can celebrate in
a communal way. The small cures are personal—as is the
Duck Lake walk and private prayer—allowing each pilgrim
to assert his individuality within the ritual. Joseph Greyeyes
never saw the need to report the end of his stomach trouble to
the shrine authorities; it was a small cure and a personal
triumph. But neither has he forgotten the fact that he was
cured—that he has his own personal proof of the
effectiveness of the shrine.

The ritual of Our Lady of Lourdes Shrine at St. Laurent is as complex as one is likely to find. Its significance is multi-levelled: historical, cultural, religious, magical. Its activities are many, both official and unofficial. Its functions, from religious to medical to the social, are complex and interrelated. And its impact upon the lives of the pilgrims, if unpredictable, is nevertheless important:

Father Doucette: *Oh yeah. I was greatly impressed [when young]. Well, I think the crowd of people impressed me. And also the sense of piety that there was. And there's always the sense of mystery. Like you know we'd hear the story of Mrs. Nolin, and of course we were quite familiar with the story of Lourdes, the cures at Lourdes. In those days I remember that downstairs there were boots and canes that were hanging, and, you know, the story of those that had been officially cured—people who had seen them, who had witnessed these cures. So that this always sort of captures the imagination of a young person. And I think that it played a great role in my faith and also in my decision to become a priest.*

5

Lace-Making:
A Family Craft Tradition

The romantic image of craftsmen and craftswomen is a pleasant one: the solitary worker surrounded by well-worn tools and carefully-chosen materials; one who has an ingrained sense of pattern and design, and an understanding of "process" which makes even the most intricate and difficult crafts appear simple in the making. Those who fashion wood, metal, stone, clay, cloth or hide into either practical or artistic items represent a class of talented people whose work, if not essential in this age of mass production, is certainly highly valued. Indeed because the Industrial Revolution made the work of artisans less a necessity and more a novelty, many crafts have been lost and the number of these people performing any one skill has decreased sharply in the last two hundred years. Yet because of the rarity and novelty of the crafts and the artisans who have survived, society values them all the more.

However, this image, although correct in many respects, is still a romantic one. Artisans, rather than being solitary workers, might rely on those around them for ideas and for help in the process of the craft. Although some of the patterns and designs might represent old, time-worn ideas, artisans can as easily include new and innovative ideas in their work. As well, since the Industrial Revolution has changed the function of craftsmanship so radically, the traditional relationship between the maker of an object and its buyer has also changed; indeed many craftsmen and craftswomen now make items simply for the sake of the craft or for their own enjoyment, without any thought of displaying or selling their work.

Mariette Buydens, a lace-maker from Hudson Bay,

represents the craftswoman of the modern age. Although, as we shall see, her work springs from an age-old Flemish tradition, the way she learned her craft, the way she works at her craft, the patterns she uses, and the use and display of her finished pieces have their foundations in modern, New World craftmanship. Indeed identifying Mrs. Buydens as a "lace-maker" seems anachronistic, since she has many other talents and responsibilities within her family circle; lace-making takes up only a small portion of her time. Furthermore, as we discover more and more about her skills, we might wonder whether she is simply a lace-maker or perhaps, more correctly, the chief artisan in a lace-making family.

But before investigating Mariette's skills, we must see her within the context of her family and understand what kind of family the Buydens are. The Buydens are descended from Belgian-Flemish immigrants to Manitoba. Marcel Buydens was born in St. Alphonse, Manitoba, in 1924, and his wife Mariette was born in the neighboring village of Bruxelles in 1926. They both spent their youth within this Flemish-Manitoban enclave and, as a result, they are fluent in Flemish and carry on many Old World Flemish traditions. The Buydens lived in a number of communities in southern and western Manitoba before settling in Hudson Bay, Saskatchewan.

Mariette and Marcel's three children, Ed, Linda, and Brian, are now adults, but the family remains very close-knit. The Buydens moved their two houses from Manitoba to Hudson Bay where they have some property on the outskirts of town, and Ed and his wife and children live next door to Mariette and Marcel on this property. Brian is a student at the University of Saskatchewan, but he still lives at his parents' home when classes are not in session. Linda and her husband live in town, but she visits her parents regularly. In addition, all members of the family, except Mariette, work either full-time or part-time at an alfalfa dehydrating plant in Hudson Bay. Thus, the family bonds remain tight and are constantly reinforced by the workaday context of the lives of the family members.

This workaday world of the Buydens might best be described as agricultural-mechanical. Their work at the alfalfa plant is but one indication of this occupational bent. Beyond this work, the Buydens are adept at the mechanical repair of cars, trucks, farm machinery, and many other contraptions of the modern age. The many cars, tractors, trucks, and bits of machinery strewn about their property is evidence of their interests and skills. In keeping with this agricultural-mechanical work, Marcel sometimes travels to farms in the area to sharpen discs for farmers who are about to begin their spring seeding. In addition, the Buydens hope to do some farming themselves, once they have drained and prepared their land. In the meantime, they keep goats on the property.

But the common bond which unites this family group extends beyond their occupations. Whether consciously or unconsciously, each member of the Buydens family has become the "expert" in one or another form of creativity; together, the family is a highly creative and expressive group, and the forms of expression which the Buydens practise range from verbal to material folklore. One explanation for the high level of artistic expression in this family is that their homestead has few modern conveniences: there is no electricity or running water. Although the Buydens take no pride in doing without these conveniences (they hope to have water and electricity sometime in the near future), their situation forces them to be self-reliant and resourceful in their forms of entertainment and artistry.

Without television and with the inconvenience of reading by kerosene lamps or by the uneven lighting from a gasoline generator, much of their time is spent in conversation. A visitor to the home immediately becomes aware of the high level of verbal interaction normal in the Buydens household. But their expressiveness is not simply a function of the present state of their household; their abiding interest in their ethnic roots and their innate "sense of family" are by far the more important factors. The Buydens are creative because they are conscious of their heritage and, even more importantly, because they are comfortable with their heritage. Thus, Mariette makes lace not simply because it is a part of her Flemish heritage to do so but because such a skill seems a natural and pleasant skill—a craft which answers her personal artistic and aesthetic sense. However, in turn, her artistic sensibilities have been shaped by her Flemish-Canadian background.

What are the different kinds of "expertise" exhibited by family members? Marcel is certainly the master of Flemish verbal traditions. He seems to have the best grasp on the Flemish dialect—a dialect which, he points out, is different from that now spoken in Belgium. His wife and children also speak, or at least understand, Flemish, but he is the acknowledged expert on the language. But beyond this knowledge, Marcel is the keeper of Flemish stories and songs. He knows many traditional stories which he can tell in either Flemish or English, and he has a repertoire of Flemish songs, some of which are hundreds of years old. Marcel is also a storehouse of information on Flemish and Flemish-Canadian traditions which, although no longer practised, are nevertheless a part of the heritage of the family.

Marcel, of course, is also adept at mechanical repairs, but his oldest son, Ed, seems to be the acknowledged jack-of-all-trades in the family. Ed is an improviser, a fixer and mechanic, an inventor whose main form of self-expression is in the practical arts. He can describe the function and potential of every bit of machinery on the property and can expound on such matters as the application of wind power, the workings of a steam punch, or the principles of the lever. His ideas for improving the homestead are boundless as is his inquisitive nature. However, Ed also shares some of his father's verbal expertise. He too knows Flemish and has his opinions on the derivation of Flemish terms and the use of Flemish in Canada. He can also tell his father's stories and will invariably pass down this tradition to his children.

Brian's expertise might be termed more academic or artistic. He is the only member of the family who has attended university, and his general knowledge of the liberal arts is prized by the family. He is the acknowledged "reader" of the family; that is, although all the Buydens are quite literate, Brian is the most voracious reader of them all. Brian is also a musician: he plays the guitar and an old pump organ in his parents' home. As well, he sings—a talent he shares with his father—although his repertoire of songs is probably quite different from Marcel's, since his Flemish is not as good as that of his father or brother. Perhaps related to his musical skills is his mathematical ability—his university interests are mathematics and computers. However, his skill for "figuring" has a practical purpose, as we shall see.

Linda seems to share less in the verbal or practical skills of her father or brothers. However, she is definitely the "family historian." She has made a study of the Buydens family and is trying to fill in the blanks in the Buydens family tree. She has ready information on places and dates of birth of past and present generations of Buydens and can tell stories of some of the more interesting members of the family. Like her father, she has a certain sense of the ethnic traditions of the Flemish-Canadians, but she seems to distance herself a bit from these traditions—as one might expect of an historian.

Despite these various areas of expertise, however, there is a considerable overlap of talents among the family members. Although Marcel and Ed are versed in the practical arts, Brian also shares in these mechanical skills. Although Brian is the family musician, his father plays the accordion and thus shares Brian's talents in that area. Everyone knows the stories which Marcel tells, and all are capable of retelling them although perhaps not with the same skill as Marcel or Ed. Likewise, every Buydens has a sense of family history, and thus all of the family members have been good sources for Linda. But as we shall see, this overlap of skills and interests plays a vital part in the total creativity of these people. The expertise of one family member is reinforced and encouraged by the knowledge of the others.

Where does Mariette fit in? She too knows the Flemish language very well and can share both stories and songs with her husband. She too is a source for family history. But her expertise lies in crafts. While her husband and sons tinker with machinery, she tinkers with cloth for her skills involve the practical and artistic use of thread and textile:

Linda: *My mother also does some crocheting. She does thread embroidery—*
Brian: *Knitting.*
Linda: *Yes.*
Ed: *Liquid embroidery.*
Linda: *Yeah, she does thread embroidery, she does liquid embroidery.*

116

Brian: *She also does housework—[laughter].*[1]

Her children might also have mentioned that Mariette makes hooked rugs and quilts. In general, she "makes things" out of cloth; extra bits of fabric and old clothes demand Mariette's skills in this area:

Taft: *Well which [craft] did you like to do better? Is there one you prefer?*
Mariette: *Oh, I think I like that [lace-making] better.*
Taft: *You like lace better.*
Mariette: *Yeah, but you get to the point that you sort of get tired of doing that all the time. That's when you switch to this [other crafts].*
Ed: *She didn't enjoy doing it [other crafts] as much, but she enjoyed looking at it.*
Marcel: *Well, you see, it was . . . what we had the most of. You see, if we got too many scraps [of cloth], well then we got rugs and quilts.*
Taft: *Oh, you make quilts too?*
Mariette: *First the quilts, and then the little leftovers [of material] went in here [the rugs], you see. . . .*
Marcel: *You see, it's just like Canada Packers and the pigs. You use everything that's on the pig—even the squeal, if they could get it [laughter].*

But, as Mariette admits, her favourite craft is lace-making, and it is this craft which, more than any other, makes her rather special in the context of Saskatchewan folklore: there are many quilt-makers and rug-hookers in the province but scarcely anyone else adept at making lace in the traditional Belgian manner.

The process of making lace involves two basic steps: making a net out of thread, and weaving thread through the holes of the net to create a design—this second process is called filling-in or, in the Buydens' Flemish, "filleting." Making the net involves the same process used to construct fishing nets, as Marcel and Ed explain:

Ed: *Well, this is a fisherman's net—that is a fisherman's net.*
Marcel: *It's a fisherman's* knot, *not a fisherman's net.*
Ed: *No, it's not the same net.*

Marcel's correction of his son's description is important: the same knots used by fishermen in the construction of their nets are used by lace-makers, but the resulting lace netting in no way functions like a fisherman's net. The relationship, however, between lace-making and net-making is not lost on the Buydens, and they agree that the probable origin of lace-making was in the ancient craft of the fisherman. Interestingly, the Buydens own a small fresh-water fishing net which Mariette fashioned using her lace-making skills.

Making the net is by far the simpler of the two steps, but it is not as easy a task as it appears:

Taft: *Now do you start it on a frame?*
Marcel & Linda: *No, no.*
Linda: *On a chair.*
Marcel: *Oh a chair or a doorknob or anything.*
Ed: *You make one slip knot. Then you add a knot to it.*

The trick isn't in making the knot—a simple process in itself—but in keeping each square of the netting in the same proportion as every other square, for in lace-making, precision is very important. Mariette's main tool for both steps of the process is a long, thin "needle," which is actually a bobbin or shuttle for holding the lacing thread and directing the thread during the knotting or weaving processes. In making the net, however, Mariette also employs a wooden dowl which acts as a gauge for the size of the netting square: the larger the dowl, the larger the square. Yet these tools are not all that is necessary for this kind of precise work; while she makes the net, Mariette must apply a constant pressure to the netting so that the thread is always stretched the same distance with every tying of the knot. Otherwise, when the netting is finished, the different pressures applied to the thread will show themselves in different dimensions to the individual netting squares, regardless of the size of the wooden dowl. Mariette begins her

118

netting at one corner of the piece, first making one square, then two, then three and so on, until she creates a triangular piece of netting; then she works in reverse order, making (for example) fifty squares, then forty-nine, and so on, until she has worked back down to one square. This process produces a diamond-shaped net, or, when removed from the chair-rung or doorknob, a square or rectangular piece of netting.

Filling-in is the next step. Before Mariette can weave the design onto the netting, she must place the net onto a frame, "just like stretching a beaver skin," as Marcel explains. The frame has a moveable side so that different lengths of netting can be attached to it; in this respect, the frame is a smaller version of a quilting frame. The edges of the frame contain a series of holes through which thread is passed to temporarily lash the net firmly and evenly to the four sides of the frame. When filling-in, Mariette prefers to lay the frame flat on top of the kitchen table, although she admits that other lace-makers might prefer to work with the frame slanted or upright—whichever is comfortable.

Once the net is on the frame, Mariette's weaving can begin. The first step, however, involves a quick check of the calculations which she made before she began the lace-making process. As Marcel explains, "The first thing she does . . . after she got it on the frame, she starts counting the holes to see how many holes she got." Each hole in the net serves a purpose, either to be filled in or to be left as it is, so that the design will be apparent on the background of the netting. When she is satisfied that the number of holes corresponds to the overall design which she has in mind, she begins the weaving process: "You start in the middle [of the design] and that way you have your pattern nicely centred," says Mariette.

The filling-in has the quality of a large, mathematical puzzle. The lace-maker must calculate in advance where every stitch in the weaving will lead in terms of the overall pattern. A good lace-maker will use the thread on the needle as economically as possible, not backtracking to fill in a hole with more than the requisite amount of thread, nor working herself into a corner where the thread must be cut and knotted and the design begun again on a different section of the netting:

Making the netting

Filling in on the frame

120

Brian: *It's something like—you seen the little house you got to draw without lifting your pencil off?*
Taft: *Yeah.*
Brian: *Well you can't lift your thread up, so you got to draw the thing without lifting your thread up. You see?*
Taft: *I see. So you have to figure out a sort of pattern.*
Brian & Ed: *Yeah.*
Brian: *Where you're going to go next.*
Mariette: *You have to choose . . .*
Taft: *Then the only way that you can ever get out of where you're heading to—*
Ed: *—is to knot it off.*
Brian: *You can sometimes circle back, but you don't like to do that too often, because, you know, some person sitting there with a magnifying glass will see where you did it. Or you can just knot it off and start somewhere else again. You know, you don't like to put too many knots in there either.*
Ed: *The knots have to be hidden, eh?*

Thus, the filling-in requires some planning and calculation before the work can begin. Although older practitioners of this craft might have done such calculations in their heads, Mariette makes use of a more modern method—precision takes precedence over tradition here. Since fillng-in is a kind of mathematical puzzle, the design can be worked out on graph paper. Each square on the graph paper represents a square on the netting, and by using a pencil, Mariette can discover the best strategy for creating the design before actually bending over the frame. While she admires the ability of past lace-makers to work from instinct or from quick mental calculations, Mariette sees no reason to follow this traditional path since using graph paper works so efficiently.

However, Mariette's innovations belie the traditional training which she received in lace-making. Her teacher was Mrs. Rachel Mannens, a Flemish immigrant who was born in Belgium in 1900 and who died in Mariette's home town of Bruxelles in 1951. Her skill at lace-making was well-known throughout the Flemish community in southern Manitoba, and her craft was evident from the decor of her home:

Mariette: *She had curtains on her windows from the lace.*
She had a table cloth on her table and she had runners on her
cupboard.
Ed: *How about a bedspread? Didn't she have a bedspread?*
Mariette: *No, she was making one when she died. She had*
one. She made one for her daughter, but she didn't have any
[for herself]. I never [saw it]. That was packed away.
Brian: *I know she had a piece that was done when she died.*

But Mrs. Mannens herself deviated from the craft
tradition as practiced in Belgium. There, one worker would
make the netting, while another would do the filling-in:

Mariette: *But in Belgium, people made it and they used to*
sell it.
Ed: *Like cottage industries and that, eh? They'd have a*
bunch of people filling in the nets. And sales people. . . . I
guess you'd call it a cottage industry, eh?
Mariette: *About the same as our clothing industries where*
you do piecework. You know, everybody has certain pieces
that—
Ed: *What was it? She [Mrs. Mannens] had a sister or*
something that could only do nets?
Mariette: *That's right.*
Ed: *And she didn't know how to fill them in, so she'd get this*
lady [Mrs. Mannens] to fill them in. [. . .]
Ed: *Now this lady [Mrs. Mannens], I think, in Belgium used*
to fill in all the time. But she was determined that she was
going to learn the whole trade, so you know, whatever, she
could do the whole thing. While her sister—what relation
was that?
Mariette: *Sister-in-law.*
Ed: *Sister-in-law could only [do the netting]. See, that's the*
reason why it's dying, eh?
Mariette: *And if she wanted to get a nice piece of lace, she*
had to make sure she was good friends with this other lady
[Mrs. Mannens], or she didn't get nowhere. Whereas this
other lady, she could do it just like I'm able to do it.

Essentially, Mrs. Mannens adapted her skills to the situation in which she found herself as an immigrant to Canada. In Manitoba, there was no established lace-making industry; the specialization of a highly commercial and well-organized craft was not to be found on the prairies. She knew that if lace-making was to survive among the immigrant Flemings, she had to know all the steps in the lace-making process. Whereas in Belgium she was a specialist in filling-in, in Manitoba she would have to be a "generalist"—that is, someone who could make nets, fill them in, and teach these skills to the next generation of lace-makers. However, as Ed implies, learning both steps in the lace-making process was doubly difficult for most students, and thus there was a much greater danger of the skill dying out in Manitoba than in Belgium.

Not that there weren't those who wanted to learn this intricate craft. As Mariette puts it, "lace was pretty well the *in* thing" in her community, and many young girls wanted to learn from Mrs. Mannens. However, the successful student must not only have enthusiasm but also the necessary disposition and self-will. Mrs. Mannens' sister-in-law obviously did not have these qualities:

Mariette: *Just making the net—this lady loved to talk—this other lady. And she used to make the nets, and to make the nets, you're able to talk. But if you're filling it in to put a pattern on it, you concentrate on counting stitches. That's why she didn't learn it—she couldn't stop talking [laughter].*

To be a total lace-maker, one had to have patience; one had to be able to concentrate entirely on the work at hand for hours on end. If one was easily distracted, impatient, or perhaps too garrulous, one would never learn the craft. But another factor in limiting the number of serious students of the art involved the New World context in which these immigrants found themselves. The influence of the other immigrant ethnic groups and the pressure of mainstream Canadian culture discouraged some girls from carrying on this Flemish tradition:

Ed: *Mrs. Mannens was the local teacher [of the craft], eh? Everybody around there learned probably from Mrs. Mannens.*

Mariette: *She was the only one in that district who was doing it, because her sister-in-law could only make nets.*

Ed: *Well her daughter made a few pieces too. But her daughter became more interested in the English arts than in the Flemish arts. Well, I should give you a little background on that. You see, the Flemish and the English were living together.*

Taft: *In this town?*

Ed: *Yeah. A little ways apart. And the Flemish farmers were always trying to be better than the English farmers and vice versa. And some of the English children would start acting like the Belgian children, because everyone wants to be what they aren't. And the Belgian children would do the same: trying to be like the English, because they figured that was better. So this girl decided that she wanted to be more English than Flemish. She didn't want to have anything to do with the Flemings or the Flemish arts, or anything like that. So she tried to become English by not doing the arts. By talking English. It didn't work, but she thought it did [laughs]. That's how the art dies, you know.*

Although it would be easy for Belgian immigrants to learn Canadian (or "English") crafts, Canadians would have had a harder time learning lace-making from Mrs. Mannens, since her language of instruction was Flemish.

But Mariette had both the desire and the disposition to learn lace-making. When she was around fifteen years old, she went to see Mrs. Mannens:

Mariette: *I remember she had told my mother that if I wanted to learn, she'd be willing to teach me. And that was right in my line. That was what I really had in mind. That was my line of work. So one day, I says to mother—it's only maybe three-quarters of a mile from our place—I said, "I'm going to go over and see her and wonder if she could show me just a little bit." I didn't have the slightest idea how it was done. So I went there and I asked her, "Are you busy?" And she said, "Why?" And I said, "Would you teach me? Just to start so I know just about what I'm heading at?" "Sure." So we sat there the whole afternoon. And she gave me a little bit of thread and she let me borrow her needle, because I didn't have a needle then of mine. . . . And when I was ready to go home, she said, "Take this needle with you and thread," and she said, "See if you can master it." And master it I did [laughs]. Sometime later, I came back and showed her how I had made the net. And she was really surprised because very few people do it. "It takes them a long time before they get on to it," she told me. She couldn't believe her eyes.*

Taft: *Had she explained how to do this to you, or did you just sort of watch?*

Mariette: *No, she did it first and then she made me do it. And she kept watching, and now and again she'd say, "Oops, I think you're making a mistake." And she'd straighten it out for me. But I managed to do it. But later on—I had made a few netting pieces—and later on I put them on a frame. Then I went to her place for a couple of days or so. Because to fill in the pattern takes more than just a quick show. You have to be there a day or two.*

Mrs. Mannens' method of teaching involved both verbal and visual instruction. Mariette had to follow carefully the stitching pattern of her teacher in order to learn the intricacies of filling-in. Mrs. Mannens would think up a pattern or design, weave one section of it on the netting, and then allow her pupil to copy the pattern on the rest of the net. Mariette's rose-pattern table cloth retains the evidence of this kind of instruction:

Taft: *Where did you get the pattern from?*

Mariette: *She [Mrs. Mannens] made it out of her head. She was fantastic. She used to put one on and then I'd have to put the others on. Everything was like that. She'd just put one on. Years ago—*

Ed: *I can demonstrate on this [the table cloth] here. She would make the one rose and told mother to make the other rose. . . .*

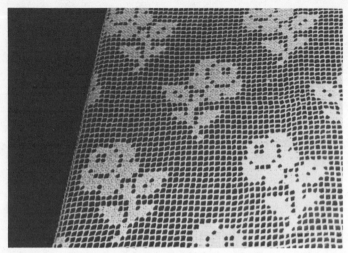

Rose-pattern tablecloth (detail)

Mariette: *Years ago, the old fashioned windows used to have lace on the window sheets. . . . I don't have the pattern. And I just loved [it]. It was a beautiful pattern. So I asked her how wide I had to make it. How many stitches. And she told me. And I just did the length of my windows. Again, I put it on my frame and walked to her place with it. While she put a pattern of each [design] on it and then I come home and I finish it.*

After her apprenticeship, Mariette started making lace pieces. As her expertise grew, so did her repertoire of different kinds of lace-work:

Linda: *Like you said, "What do you use them for?" You can decorate arm chairs, chesterfields, you know—*
Marcel: *Like you see, decorations, door panels—*
Linda: *You know, it gives you an idea—*
Marcel: *Around the [pillow] case—*
Ed: *I wanted to do most of my truck in it, but she [laughter]—*
Linda: *Even placemats. You could make placemats, if you wanted to.*
Mariette: *Borders, fancy borders for dresses, gown cuffs, all sorts of [things].*

126

Table cloths, window curtains, wall hangings, doilies to place between furniture tops and items on display (Mariette made one to fit on top of an old gramophone)—all manner of cloth items lend themselves to Mariette's lace-work. There are some projects she has yet to try, but her teacher remains the model of the complete craftswoman:

Brian: *Like, for example, one priest got a robe of this made out of it [lace].*
Mariette: *Yeah, this lady [Mrs. Mannens] was very good friends with a neighbor. And this neighbor, one of their boys went to be a priest. And when he—*
Ed: *When he was ordained—*
Mariette: *When he was ordained as a priest, here she had this nice white dress for him ready. She told me she worked on it for three winters to get it done. But it was lace. The only thing that wasn't lace was just over the shoulders and a little bit on the sleeves. The rest was all lace. I saw it. It was really nice.*

However, if Mrs. Mannens is Mariette's model for craftsmanship, she is not her sole source of inspiration for lace designs. Although when she first began the craft, she borrowed patterns from her mentor, she soon found other sources of design. She found patterns in newspapers and books and although these patterns were meant for crocheting—an allied but very different process—Mariette was able to adapt many of them to lace-making. "Home Sweet Home," "Pal," and "Puss" were all taken from these printed sources: "They looked kind of nice in the papers, so I decided to try to make them."

Perhaps her most innovative designs, however, are her "celebration" series. To mark certain milestones in Canadian history, Mariette has designed lace pieces based on the official celebration insignia: the Canadian Centennial, the Manitoba Centennial, and Saskatchewan's Seventy-Fifth Anniversary. But her inspirations do not necessarily lead to successful lace patterns. Some of the crocheting patterns simply do not lend themselves to adaptation. Likewise, not all designs are "full" enough for the medium of lace. The Manitoba Centennial is one example; Mariette could not express the thin, sparse numbers of the emblem without destroying the careful balance of filled-in and unfilled-in squares which give the lace its aesthetic form:

Mariette: *Well, all it is is just "100"—*
Linda: *It's a "one" and two zeroes with four little numbers sort of thing. . . .*
Mariette: *That's why I put it on a rug. You couldn't possibly make a nice pillow piece out of that. But Canada's Centennial you could.*
Ed: *The Saskatchewan too.*
Mariette: *Yeah, the Saskatchewan. . . .*
Mariette: *Canada's Centennial had that nice, sort of, star, like with Nova Scotia and Prince Edward Island and everything else.*
Ed: *You see, you try and fill in the nets. Otherwise you see, all you have is a number.*
Taft: *I see.*
Linda: *It's so flimsy, it's so flimsy, eh?*
Mariette: *As you fill it in, it gives it a little more body.*

Hooked rugs, including the
Manitoba Centennial

The Canadian Centennial

128

Ed: *For instance, The Dog ["Pal"] that's laying there. Did you notice how they filled the bottom holes? There's no reason for it—*
Brian: *But it just fills—*
Ed: *—except that it made the net look more complete.*
Mariette: *Yeah.*
Ed: *You put the flowers to the side and the trimming on the edge.*

Here we see the aesthetic of lace-making at work. The design must fit the net, or more accurately, it must fill *out* the net to a degree which is pleasing to the eye. Neither too many nor too few squares must be filled to achieve the proper effect. But the aesthetic goes beyond the idea of balance. As noted earlier, the lace must exhibit good craftsmanship. Every knot in the filling-in reveals a possible error in the strategy of the weave; furthermore, a knot fills in too much of the square— again, balance is all-important. Even if these errors are apparent only under a magnifying glass, as Brian suggests, they are enough to lessen the aesthetic value in the eyes of Mariette and her family.

The difficulty of the design is also a part of the aesthetic. The Manitoba Centennial was unaesthetic as a piece of lace, partly because of its sparseness but also, perhaps, because of its inherent simplicity of design. Thus, the insignia was "relegated" to the lesser craft of the hooked rug, where it does form a pattern pleasing to the eye.

The materials used in the craft are also a part of the aesthetic. Mariette's most prized items are her earliest work in which she used fine silk thread from Belgium. This multi-coloured thread hearkens back to the Old World craft, which undoubtedly adds to the appeal of these lace pieces. In addition, any knots which have to be made in the silk threads do not show as clearly as those made in the white cotton crocheting thread which she now uses. Unfortunately, Mariette can no longer find any of the Belgian thread so that she must resort to the coarser cotton thread for her lace.

There is also an aesthetic attached to the theme of the piece. Although Mariette chose some designs because they were used by Mrs. Mannens and were therefore traditional to

"Puss"

the craft, many of her other designs seem to have a domestic, family-oriented theme. Her two "Home Sweet Home" pieces certainly express this theme, as well as do the "Mother" and "Mom Dad" pillow cases. The "Pal" and "Puss" pieces also seem to speak to domesticity. This theme in Mariette's work should come as no surprise, considering how close the bonds are in the Buydens family. Indeed, her work is one manifestation of the strong ties which hold this family together.

The celebration series expresses a different aesthetic. These designs are a recent innovation in Mariette's work and seem to stem from a change in the function of the lace pieces. In trying to explain why her mother never made a "V for Victory" piece after World War II (certainly a celebration design), Linda addresses this change in function:

Linda: *No, no, she had a different reason for making it in those days. In those days she was trying to decorate the house, you know. So she was making runners for countertops. And "V for Victory" just didn't fit in there.*
Brian: *Nowadays, it's more for artistic value, you know.*
Linda: *Well yeah, like for pictures. But back then, she was using it for practical[things]. You know, the table cloth went*

130

"Pal"

on the table, the runners went on the china cupboards, the little square went on top of an old-time gramophone, you see.

In the 1940s and 1950s, lacework was a part of the practical decor of the times. Today, home decoration tends to downplay elaborate or intricate designs of the sort one finds in lacework. The very word "doily" brings to mind a grandmotherly form of decor. This change in the function of the lace is evident in the current Buydens household. Table cloths and doilies, rather than being a practical part of the interior decoration, are now kept in a trunk; they are heirlooms brought out on occasion to admire as a mark of craftsmanship and, perhaps, as a mark of the Buydens family heritage. Those pieces that are on display are literally framed as works of art; rather than being used as protection for furniture tops or embellishments on chair arms, these pieces hang on the wall or decorate the front of non-functional pillows. They are now show-pieces.

The celebration series expresses the sense of lacework as art rather than craft. Although there is undoubtedly some patriotic inspiration behind Mariette's choices, these

131

Pillow cases

Design in Belgian silk lace

insignia also represent designs of technical interest, patterns which display Mariette's quality of workmanship. If "Celebrate Saskatchewan" is more immediately meaningful as a design than is the rose-pattern on a table cloth, it is nevertheless not as practical in terms of traditional household decor. The piece is to be viewed rather than used.

Of course, the trend away from practicality began when the first lace-maker left Belgium to settle in Canada. The mass production of lace patterns for commercial trade was nothing if not practical, whereas the Flemish immigrant's craft was a more personal and private expression. Instead of being a full-time occupation, lace-making became a hobby, even for a master craftswoman like Mrs. Mannens. In discussing the lace surplice which took Mrs. Mannens three winters to complete, this point came up:

Taft: *And that would take quite a while to do?*
Mariette: *Three winters. And she was fast at it because she had done it for years in Belgium.*
Linda: *Well, this was just at the end of the day, you know. They carried on housework during the day and then in the evenings, instead of watching television [which they didn't have], they sat and did this. So that's why it took three winters. . . . They didn't work from eight o'clock in the morning till eight o'clock at night, sort of thing, like they would have in Belgium in a working place.*
Brian: *Yeah, you see, they weren't making a living at it, eh?*
Taft: *This was just on the side?*
Linda: *Yeah, yeah, this was in the evening as a hobby, relaxing.*
Ed: *But in Belgium, they were paid per piece.*

Mariette considers her craft a "hobby" and gives it the same priority in her daily schedule as did her teacher:

Linda: *And usually in the wintertime too.*
Brian: *Wintertime, yes.*
Taft: *Why usually in the winter?*
Linda: *Because there was nothing else to do.*
Mariette: *Too cold to go outside [laughter].*

Brian: *It's like even the farmers here; you know, if you're a farmer, you have most of your [free] time in the winter, eh?*
Mariette: *No gardening in the winter, nothing—and too cold to go out.*

Less time spent on lace-making meant that the craftswoman would make fewer pieces than her Belgian counterpart. Each piece, therefore, became much more valuable because of the relative scarcity of this Canadian-made lace and because of the total amount of time taken over each piece. As a result, each piece of lace became a major project for the lace-maker, a project worth extra deliberation, extra care, and ultimately extra artistry, if such a piece was worth doing at all. Without the commercial incentive for making lace, the entire function and aesthetic of the craft could not help but change.

Thus, neither Mrs. Mannens nor Mariette would ever consider selling their work—the pieces are simply too valuable to sell:

Ed: *She's been asked to sell them, but how can you put a price on them?*
Mariette: *In order to put a price on them, you'd have to charge too much because they're too much work. If you were to charge by the hour, people would never pay it.*
Ed: *Well they might, but only for the artistic value of it. And then even, like being paid per hour, you might be way too low on your price.*
Mariette: *Although I have had some people say to me, "Name your price," but I never did do that.*

Instead of selling their work, such artisans keep them within the immediate family, perhaps displaying them on the walls of the home, as Mariette does, or on rare occasions giving pieces as gifts to other family members or to close friends.

However, if Mariette would not sell her pieces, she still wanted some way of displaying her craft to those outside of her immediate family. The compromise between selling one's work and keeping it hidden away from public view is the local fair or craft contest. Like many other Saskatchewan craftswomen. Mariette chose this avenue to bring her skills to the attention of her neighbors:

Mariette: *Well I lived in a town close to the fairgrounds. And from my yard, you could see the fair. And I decided that, well, we were going to go to the fair. So usually, when you go to the fair, you spend money there. I decided, well instead of spending money, maybe I'll make a little bit. So I entered a whole lot of them [pieces of lace], and I made more on the fair than what I spent [laughs].*
Ed: *Winning prizes.*
Taft: *Winning prizes?*
Ed: *She won prizes all the time. She never went to a fair without winning a prize.*
Marcel: *That's because it [the lace] was the only thing of its kind.*
Mariette: *That's right. And because I entered [a piece], I didn't have to pay my way in. I got my free ticket. So I came in there even.*
Marcel: *She took in three pieces—she had first, second, and third [prizes].*
Taft: *No one else was doing this?*
Linda: *That's right.*
Ed: *Not to our knowledge.*
Linda: *By this time, when she was entering them, the other lady [Mrs. Mannens] had passed away a few years earlier.*

Indeed the craft fair is the perfect compromise. Mariette could keep her work but still earn some money; she could receive public acclaim due a craftswoman of her ability without having to sell her work.

Like Mrs. Mannens before her, Mariette is now an artisan-teacher of lace-making. In the natural evolution of any artisan, she began as an apprentice, went on to become a craftswoman in her own right, and now has the responsibility of passing on her specialized knowledge to others. As one might expect, her students are members of her own family. Indeed it is difficult to ignore the other members of the Buydens family when exploring Mariette's craft for they have always played some part in the making of lace. For example, she has always found her equipment impossible to buy and has had to rely on the practical skills of her father, her husband, and her sons:

Taft: *Where'd you get your frame?*
Mariette: *First I borrowed hers [Mrs. Mannens] and then my dad made me one. And when moving, I lost it. And then this one here, my husband made.*

Her needles were also borrowed and then home-made, but with less success. Mariette has never been able to find the proper lace-making needle in Canadian stores; fortunately, though, through Mrs. Mannens she was able to get two precious needles in 1941, which she still has and uses. However Ed, being the family expert in the practical arts, has taken on the challenge of supplying more of these needles:

Ed: *I made the hooks for rugs. That's what I do. That's why my lacework is way behind my brother's. For instance, he makes the patterns and he makes some of the lace, whereas I was busy trying to make needles. I can make a needle [for lace]. The only thing I can't do is temper it so it's spring steel. So after a couple of—*
Mariette: *If bad was come to worse, what he makes, I can do [with].*
Taft: *So you actually make the lace needle?*
Brian: *But it doesn't last nearly as long—*
Ed: *Because it's not spring steel—*
Brian: *[It only lasts] one of these nets or so.*
Ed: *Yeah, one of mine would last about three or four nets—*
Taft: *When you say "last," what happens to them?*
Ed: *Well they bend, eh?*
Brian: *You know, there's—*
Ed: *As you're working the needle, you're bending it back and forth, and the iron I'm using gets tired.*
Brian: *Metal fatigue, they call it.*
Ed: *Yeah, it breaks.*

But the family participates in lace-making in a more direct fashion as well. Mariette's three children have all learned the basics of lace-making, at least enough to be able to make the netting. However, their "apprenticeship" was not as self-motivated as was Mariette's:

Taft: *The three of you learned from your mother how to do this?*
Brian: *Yeah.*
Linda: *No.*
Brian: *Sort of, sort of.*

The responses of Brian and Linda represent a different attitude towards the craft from that of their mother. The three children see lace-making as an important family and ethnic tradition, but their personal commitment to becoming lace-makers varies from sibling to sibling:

Brian: *She [Mariette] said, "Well here's the net and here's the needle."*
Ed: *Well basically me and Brian were—and Linda too—we were afraid it was going to die.*
Linda: *Well it's children's curiosity too. When we were the age of her there [pointing to Ed's four year old daughter], we just used to ask, "What are you doing?" you know.*

Brian has been the most avid pupil and has gone the farthest in his lace-making education:

Taft: *Well Brian, when did you take it up?*
Brian: *When? Oh, a few years ago.*
Taft: *Was it after Ed?*
Ed: *No, it was before me.*
Linda: *After me and before Ed.*
Brian: *The trouble was, I was too curious, you see. Like I don't know, it just seemed to be the thing to do at the time. Mind you, I don't think I can make a piece right now. I could make the nets, but the filling-in, for some reason—mother showed me, you know. It takes about five minutes and I know what I'm doing again, eh? And then it leaves.*
Ed: *It pops right out of your mind.*
Brian: *It pops right out of your—*
Linda: *It leaves—*
Brian: *It's just like—I don't know. You just forget.*

Linda: *I found the weaving part the hardest—the filling-in. I really—oh, that was just—*

As Linda says, the filling-in is the most difficult step and the one which takes the most perseverance. The observation of all three that the technique "pops" out of one's mind indicates how single-minded the lace-maker must be; learning the craft is not enough—the trick is to stay with it constantly until the process becomes second-nature. Unlike Brian, Linda has not continued with the craft, and she explains her cryptic answer to my earlier question in this fashion:

Linda: *Actually, some of us didn't learn from our mother. Some of us just made a desperate attempt and then quit [laughter]. You see, we were living in this house when she was teaching us. I was sitting here on this bench. Every time I made a mistake, she went over and tried to correct me. I'd be muttering under my breath unprintable adjectives. So finally, I just gave it up, you know. . . . I guess I must have been like the other lady—I wanted to talk too much [laughter].*

Linda is interested in the craft as an expression of the family's ethnic heritage, but she does not have the proper inclination or disposition for the kind of work lace-making demands.

As Ed implied, he has been too busy with the practical side of making tools for his mother's work to learn lace-making. But he is now learning the skill and in all probability will be the major disseminator of this tradition to future generations. His great interest in preserving family traditions and his tendency to "tinker," as well as the fact that he lives next door to his mother and that he is committed to living and working on the family property, make him the best candidate for carrying on this craft.

But the fact that all of the children know how to do the netting, if not the filling-in, means that they can all contribute to the pieces on which their mother is working. The very fact that they show an interest in the craft encourages Mariette to continue her work. However, her children can also relieve her of the more monotonous task of netting, and in the case of Brian, even the job of weaving itself:

Brian: *Well what will often happen is that I'll go over to see what she's done, eh? And I'll say, "Come on ma, you got to keep working." And she'll say, "Oh no, I'm getting tired now." "Well then, show me." It's the same old thing, I guess. You know, then you'll go for a while.*

It is indeed "the same old thing." Just as Mrs. Mannens would start a piece and then let Mariette continue, now Mariette will start a pattern and then let her son continue. In this respect, then, the actual maker of the piece of lace is sometimes problematical: the design might come from a crocheting book; Ed or Linda might make the netting; Mariette might do much of the filling-in, but Brian might take over from time to time when his mother is tired or otherwise occupied.

Peacock design

But the communal nature of the work goes beyond the physical task of turning thread into lace. All of the children are also involved in the planning of a piece. Again, Brian, because of his mathematical interests, seems to take the lead here, but it is not uncommon for Mariette and her children to sit down with pieces of graph paper in order to work out the best strategy for the filling-in:

Taft: *Well now, when you want to make a new design then, Brian maps it out for you? Is that how it works?*
Brian: *Unless it exists already. But sometimes she makes her own—*
Linda: *I think it was me and you [Brian] who did the centennial, eh?*
Brian: *Yeah.*
Linda: *And I did the Expo one and you did the Saskatchewan one. Well we all tried to take a turn at it, really.*
Ed: *They sit around the table and make one.*
Linda: *Everybody grabs a hold of a piece of graph paper. Whichever one looks the best, you know, is the one that gets picked.*
Ed: *And then someone says, "Well, no, it would look better if we put in more spaces here or if we added this here."*

The communal nature of the Buydens' lace-making is a strong indication of how viable this tradition is in this family. Rather than the work of a solitary craftsman, the Buydens' lace-making is the result of one acknowledged expert, others which make the skill possible (frame and needle-making), and willing apprentices. From the initial stage of selecting a pattern and planning the filling-in to the netting and finally to the weaving, there is no one member of the family who is entirely responsible for the work.

Perhaps one mark of the communal nature of this work is the fact that Mariette's children seem far more articulate than Mariette herself when explaining the craft. One would expect an expert to be the best source of description and opinion on lace-making, but this is not always the case with material folklore. As noted earlier, the master craftsperson's work becomes second-nature or instinctual: there is no need

Furniture protector

for the truly talented artisan to be conscious of every step in the process. Thus, many artisans cannot explain the process of their craft very well; it is too ingrained, too inexpressible in words. After all, the very nature of material folklore is that it is a form of creativity or expression which does not use or need language.

Mariette's children marvel at how quickly and smoothly their mother works; she does not have to think about every stitch. They, however, are merely apprentices; they have not yet learned to perform the craft as though there were born with the knowledge. Thus, because they must still be aware of every stitch and be conscious of their progress at all times, Mariette's children are best able to talk about the craft. As students of lace-making, they are continually "translating" what they observe from their mother's work into verbal explanations and then back into non-verbal or material expression as they attempt to understand lace-making and to share their knowledge among themselves. As they become more proficient at lace-making, as their skills become more ingrained, they too might lose the ability to verbalize their craft.

But the communal nature of the craft is also indicative of the communal nature of the people who make up the family. Lace-making is one more bond for the Buydens, and it is a bond which is likely to last into the next generation:

Taft: *So you're going to pass this on?*

Ed: *Oh—*

Linda: *We're hoping to.*

Ed: *That's one reason why I'm learning it.*

Brian: *We hate like heck to see it die. You know, it would be just so unfortunate, I think.*

Ed: *So if I can only learn enough of it to pass it on, I'll be happy with it.*

6

Conclusion

These three studies of Saskatchewan folklore can only represent in a small way the vast storehouse of provincial tradition. They are simply three examples. However, in their characteristics and qualities, these three studies are representative of many of the aspects of folklore discussed in the first chapters. In their separate ways, the storytelling, the pilgrimage, and the lace-making teach us what folklore is all about.

In these three studies, we clearly see four of the divisions of folklore outlined at the beginning of the book. The storytelling is a prime example of verbal folklore; the pilgrimage is nothing if not a ritual; and the making of lace is a good example of both the art and craft aspects of material folklore. Belief pervades all three examples, showing itself most clearly in the St. Laurent pilgrimage. There we see manifestations of religious belief, medical belief, and perhaps even magical belief. However, in more subtle ways, belief showed itself at the storytelling session: what the ranchers considered "true" gives us clues about their world views; their stories about local characters indicate something of their social beliefs—what is and what is not acceptable or normal behaviour in their community; the stories which Carl and Helga tell on each other reveal something of how they view farm life and family.

But these examples also tell us much about Saskatchewan folklore in general. Considering the great ethnic mix of people in this province, it is not surprising that the traditions explored in these case studies echo those of the English, French, Cree, Metis, Danish, German, and Flemish cultures. Similarly, these three examples show how the folklore of other cultures and world-wide traditions become localized and thus a part of Saskatchewan's unique heritage. The ranchers' stories are, with one exception, home-grown tales, yet the themes of their stories are traditional among many groups of people. Hunting stories about abundant game and clever animals are told the world over. The stories of foolish and clever acts have their counterparts among all peoples. Are there any cultures in which extraordinary weather is not a topic of tales? Thus, the storytelling session demonstrates the paradox of folklore being both local and international at the same time. Of course, Carl's tall tale demonstrates the paradox in reverse, showing how an internationally-known tale can be adapted to the Saskatchewan setting.

The pilgrimage to St. Laurent is an excellent example of the mixture of local and international traditions. Just as Jeannine Lebastard adapted "Little Marian Parker" and Carl told his own variant of the heavy clay tall tale, Brother Piquet "localized" the healing ritual of Lourdes of France to a Saskatchewan setting and culture. The St. Laurent shrine shares many traditions with its counterparts in other areas of the world—the Stations of the Cross, the special healing service, the blessing of the water, the stories of cures—but it is also different from these other shrines in its adaptations and in its reflections of Saskatchewan culture. Thus, its masses in Cree, its relationship to the history of the province, and even its natural setting along the South Saskatchewan River make this pilgrimage a unique ritual in Christendom.

The Buydens' lace-making skills are a study in adaptation. Although the craft grew out of Belgian-Flemish traditions, its New World adaptations make it a unique form of material folklore. These adaptations include the change in function of lace-making from a cottage industry to a wintertime hobby, a change in manufacturing techniques from the separation of skills in Belgium to the amalgamation of skills (netting and filling-in) in the New World. The designs also show adaptation and localization: would a Belgian lace-maker create a Celebrate Saskatchewan piece? For that matter, would the specialized, commerical lace-making of Belgium allow the kind of experimentation in using crocheting patterns which is commonplace in the Buydens' work? Thus, Saskatchewan lace-making, like storytelling and attending rituals in the province, is marked by the culture in which it is found.

These three case studies also alert us to the fact that folklore is a part of all our lives. Although some folklore skills take special talents, others are practised by all of us on a daily basis. Thus, the examples run the spectrum from everyday storytelling to the highly specialized skills of Mariette Buydens. The ranchers from Borden are indeed good storytellers, but their talent is shared by many people, and the neighborly house visit is an occasion with which we are all familiar and in which we have all participated, both as talkers and listeners.

The pilgrims to St. Laurent need no special skills at all; their devotion and belief are enough for them to participate in the complex and highly symbolic ritual of the shrine. Likewise, all of us participate in rituals without any thought that we are engaged in a sophisticated form of creativity. Folklore, in the form of storytelling, playing games, humming tunes, participating in a ritual, and engaging in many other activities, is an unobtrusive yet creative and expressive part of all our lives. At the other end of the spectrum, however, is the example of lace-making. In this case study, we learn that some forms of folklore take extraordinary talent and that there are people in every culture who are "specialists" in some form of folklore: great raconteurs, singers with large repertoires, healers with special knowledge and abilities for curing diseases, painters with a skilled eye for landscape, woodcarvers whose pieces are in high demand at craft fairs.

Thus we see the many paradoxes of folklore through these case studies: an expressive form which is unique and traditional at the same time, an art which is at once both old and new, a creativity which is as regional as it is international, a skill which is both commonplace and extraordinary. And it is these very paradoxes which make folklore so fascinating. Although the paradoxical nature of folklore can be frustrating at times, its infinite complexity and infinite simplicity are a delight for the mind and the senses.

I hope that this book is frustrating for other reasons. I hope that the reader grumbles that his ethnic group was ignored, or that so-and-so tells much better stories or sings better songs than those chosen for this book. In short, I hope that the reader becomes angry because so much is left out of this book. Good. Out of such grumblings should come many other collections and studies of the folklore of Saskatchewan. The province has more folklore than can be discovered in a lifetime.

Footnotes

[1] This and all songs sung by Jeanine Lebastard were recorded in her home in Eastend on 21 July 1981. Her husband, Henri, has recently compiled a book of her songs, *Songs of Yesteryears* (Eastend: Henri Lebastard, [1982]). "Marian Parker" is documented in G. Malcolm Laws, Jr., *Native American Balladry: A Descriptive Study and a Bibliographical Syllabus*, revised ed. (Philadelphia: American Folklore Society, 1964), as F33 under "Murder Ballads."

[2] Taken from the "Old Favourites" song column, *Family Herald and Weekly Star*, 15 May 1940. Another version of this song appears in Edith Fowke and Alan Mills, *Canada's Story in Song* (Toronto: Gage, n.d.), pp. 147-49.

[3] Recorded by Barbara Cass-Beggs in 1958. Saskatchewan Archives Board accession numbers A1703-A1709. This same version appears on Cass-Beggs' *Folksongs of Saskatchewan*, Folkways Records album FE-4312 (New York: Folkways Records & Service Corp., 1963), and in Fowke and Mills, pp. 150-51.

[4] Taken from Roger L. Welsch, *The Summer It Rained: Water and Plains Pioneer Humor* (Lincoln: Nebraska Water Resources Center, Univ. of Nebraska, 1978), p. 9.

[5] Recorded by Cass-Beggs from Jim Young of Regina, probably in the late 1950s, and printed in Barbara Cass-Beggs, *Eight Songs of Saskatchewan* (Toronto: Canadian Music Sales Corp. Ltd., 1963), pp. 8-9. This same version also appears on Cass-Beggs, *Folksongs of Saskatchewan*, and in Fowke and Mills, pp. 210-11.

[6] Other versions of this song, each extolling the virtues of a specific locality, are found in British Columbia and Alberta; see Philip J. Thomas, *Songs of the Pacific Northwest* (Saanichton: Hancock House, 1979), pp. 77-80.

[7] Recorded from the singing of William Bock by Barbara Cass-Beggs in Eastend in the late 1950s, Saskatchewan Archives Board accession number A1703-A1709. Other versions of this song appear in William G. Bock, *The Best of Billy Bock*, ed. John H. Archer and Robert Peterson (Saskatoon: Modern Press, 1967), pp. 110-11, where its title is "Eastend Flood—1952," and Edward McCourt, *Saskatchewan* (Toronto: Macmillan, 1968), p. 66.

[8] Words by W. J. McIntyre and music by Robert Heath, composed in Swift Current on 28 June 1950, The song and Blowtorch himself are now in the collection of the Western Development Museum.

[9] From the Cass-Beggs collection in the Saskatchewan Archives Board (see footnote 7). This same version appeared on Cass-Beggs, *Folksongs of Saskatchewan*, and different versions appeared in Bock, pp. 103-04 and McCourt, pp. 66-67.

[10] The poem and translation are taken from Linda Dégh, "Folklore of the Bekevar Community," in *Bekevar: Working Papers on a Canadian Prairie Community*, Canadian Centre for Folk Culture Studies Paper No. 31, ed. Robert Blumstock (Ottawa: National Museums of Canada, 1979), pp. 30-31. The poem in its original Hungarian follows:

160 hold földet adtak 10 dollárér
25 dollart kértek egy tehénér
5-6 dollár volt egy borju ára
Mikor hidegre fordult as idö járása
Ezer meg ezer föld mindenfele
es mindenütt a füvet termete
a szegény ember a földet felfogta
de pénze nem jutot házra deszkára
Valaki osztán kitalálta
Az erdöböl fát hordott Csinála
A többi megláta követe példájat
Egyik a másik utan Csinálta a házat
A padját szépen ki is tapasztoták
A tetejére a fel szántot Preries földet raftak
Egy ilyen háznak a meg csinálása
Bele Került 15, vagy 20 dollárba
Igaz, hogy nyáron as esö be esett
De telen volt benne igazi jó meleg
De nagy volt ezeknek a boldogsága
Mikor be költözhetek a föld teteju házba
Hálát adva érte Istenüknek. . . .

[11] Submitted by ex-Sgt. J. D. Nicholson to the *R.C.M.P. Quarterly*, 10 (1942), 95; reprinted in the Saskatchewan History and Folklore Society, *Wake the Prairie Echoes: The Mounted Police Story in Verse* (Saskatoon: Western Producer Book Service, 1974), p. 57.

[12] In Barre Toelken, *The Dynamics of Folklore* (Boston: Houghton Mifflin, 1979), pp. 57-58.

Chapter 3

[1] This and all other transcriptions are from a taped interview with the Christensens and Ingrams which I conducted in the Christensen home on 18 June 1981.

[2] This widespread tale has been collected in Arizona, Texas, and Missouri, among other places. For full documentation see Ernest W. Baughman, *Type and Motif-Index of the Folktales of England and North America* (The Hague: Mouton, 1966), X1233 (gh). and X1655.4.1*.

[3] Diefenbaker tells this same story on himself in the film *Dief!* directed by William Canning, 16mm (Montreal: National Film Board of Canada, 1981), order number 106C 0181 033.

Chapter 4

[1] For the history of St. Laurent, see *Historique du Sanctuaire et de la Mission de St-Laurent, Sask.* (Prince Albert?: n. pub., 1954?), and Michel Fortier, ed., *100 Years of Marion Echoes: Our Lady of Lourdes, St. Laurent, Sask.* (Prince Albert: Write Way Printing, 1979?). Both pamphlets are available at St. Laurent.

[2] Interviewed at the Shrine on 13 June 1981. Father Doucette was born in Duck Lake and has been associated with the shrine in one capacity or another for his entire life.

[3] *Historique du Sanctuaire*, pp. 20-22; author's translation.

[4] Interview with Joseph Greyeyes at the shrine on 15 July 1981. Joseph Greyeyes, born and still living on the Muskeg Lake Reserve, has attended the pilgrimage for fifty-six years. He is now in his late seventies.

[5] Fortier, p. 8.

[6] Interview with Sara and Fred Bouchard (pseudonyms) at the Shrine on 16 July 1981. Sara and Fred were born on the Mistawasis Reserve where they married and raised their family. Both in their sixties, they have attended the pilgrmage for over forty years.

Chapter 5

[1] All transcriptions are from an interview with the Buydens which I conducted in their home on 21 June 1981.

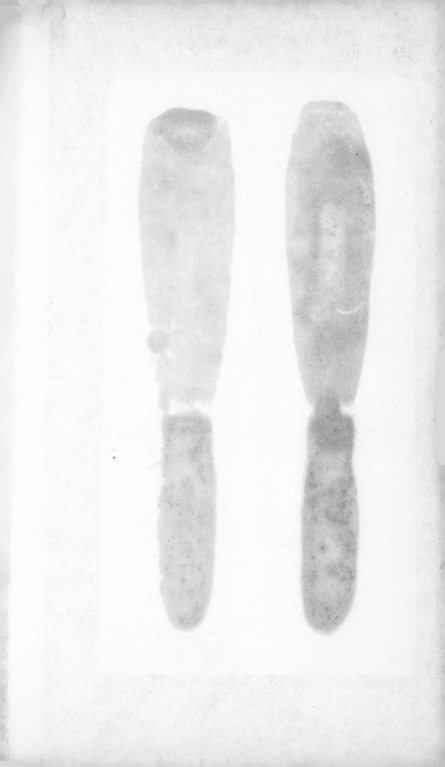